THE
MENTAL
WELLNESS
DIET

The Mental Wellness Diet

Ancient Wisdom - Evolving Science - Modern Day Options

JUSTIN BETHONEY, NP

JUSTIN BETHONEY
INTEGRATIVE PSYCHIATRY

Justin Bethoney NP IPN Inc.

First Printing, 2020

ISBN 978-0-578-74773-6
EISBN 978-0-578-74774-3

CONTENTS

~ 1 ~

INTRODUCTION: LOST ART OF MENTAL WELLNESS

Feeling Stuck?

A CANARY IN A COAL MINE

An illness is an illness is an illness, right? It sounds straightforward. If you feel pain or lose some sort of bodily function, you are ill, end of story. Yet, when it comes to mental illness, we don't think of it the same way. We tend to regard mental and emotional pain as if they aren't part of an actual illness. We think of mental and emotional pain as something different. As we are experiencing depressed moods, anxious thoughts, or chronic memory lapses, we don't say to ourselves, "Let me go see a doctor about this."

Instead, we think acknowledging these symptoms as a real illness would be an overreaction. We might feel we're complaining, or us just being weak. So, then our mental illness symptoms go on untreated. These symptoms persist, and we begin to feel like we're doing something wrong. We may ask ourselves, "How come I can't handle as much as I used to?" or "How come I don't feel as good as I used to?" or "What's wrong with me?" We might feel broken somehow. We may even feel that we are being lazy, inept, or just plain scared. But what if mental illness is actually very similar to physical illness?

You may be surprised to learn that depression, anxiety, ADHD, and even severe mental illnesses do sometimes originate in the body. Imbalances in the gut,[1-4] excess inflammation,[5-9] blood sugar regulation issues,[10-11] and nutrient deficiencies,[12-13] along with other imbalances in the body, have been shown to contribute to the development of mental illness. Mental illness can be very physical.

What's more, some research identifies depressed moods, anxiety, or mental and emotional stress as risk factors for chronic physical illnesses.[14-16] So it's true, an illness is an illness, whether mental or physical. Mental illness is very real. It's all really real.

Although everyone carries some degree of genetic predisposition (potential risk that is passed down) for mental illness, life challenges and traumas definitely play a role. Work, school, and home life stressors are major factors, as is how we make meaning out of our life experiences.

If we feel and act like we're always right and never wrong, we drive everyone around us crazy. That's probably not good for our relationships. Loneliness, lack of support, and general life dissatisfaction would tend to follow, which isn't good for our mental wellness.

If we encounter challenges but consistently feel like we've failed, then we may begin to harbor out-of-proportion fears, a sense of inadequacy, or self-hatred. In this case, we are surely headed in the direction of depression and anxiety. The way we process our experiences in life, whether it be positively or negatively, is massively impactful on our mental health.

As scientific research into mental health progresses, so evolves our understanding of how nutrition, physiology, and psychology all combine to influence our mental health. It seems as if each individual experiencing mental illness has encountered a perfect storm of toxic factors. It's usually a combination of life stress, suboptimal physical health, and some degree of toxic thinking.

Every year, research is revealing more and more about the risk factors that contribute to mental illness. Some of these environmental factors are invisible but pervasive (social media). Some are edible and seemingly unavoidable (processed/junk food). Some of these factors live in our mental landscape (imposter syndrome) and eventually poison our bodies. Others factors reside in our bodies (inflammation, gut dysbiosis, blood sugar imbalances, food sensitivities, and more) and make their way into our brains. For each of us it will be a different collection of stressors that pushes us towards mental illness.

Unfortunately, once a person finds themselves experiencing mental illness, figuring out which life stressors or factors caused us to begin to feel this way can be really difficult. When it's you, it's not so easy to quickly identify the contributing factors. It's bewildering to be struck with dark moods, pangs of anxiety, and incapacitating brain fog. Armed with this new research, however, we can now look at the development of each individual's mental illness symptoms in a unique and more informed way.

If there was a perfect expression to describe the sneaky way in which mental illness can creep up on us, it would be the old line, "it's a canary in the coal mine." This metaphor originates from the coal miner tradition of bringing caged canaries down into the dark and dusky mines. When lethal gases like carbon monoxide were unearthed, the coal miners wouldn't be able to see or smell the danger. So focused on earning a living, they'd keep digging away without realizing that they were suffocating in a lethal atmosphere. Yet, if they glanced over and saw the canary keeled over in its cage, they knew they were in danger and they needed to move quickly to the exit.

If you're working hard towards a better life for yourself and your family today, this probably sounds familiar. Many of us are digging away day in and day out, trying to build a better life for ourselves, as well as our families. Today, the canaries are the mental illness symptoms that catch our attention. Yet, unlike the coal miners, we are not as aware of what these warning signs are telling us. For many of us, instead of getting the message that we need to get out of whatever situation or thought pattern is toxic is causing us pain, we just keep digging away in hopes that maybe that pain will just go away.

There are such tight margins in our lives nowadays. We work hard to make money, but spending it is easy. So we have to go back and work more, and so continues the cycle. We can do a lot in a day, but most of it feels like busywork that never really helps us get ahead. We wish we had more time for ourselves...but spending time with ourselves seems almost foreign. When we do get 10 minutes to ourselves, it can be a real challenge to actually relax. There's often a pull to distract ourselves with something. It's like we've forgotten how to bring it down a couple notches, relax, and be with ourselves.

Life is busy, and even when it isn't, our brains are still just as busy. Our supply of time, money, energy, and patience are always in a state of drought. In some ways, life seemed easier before - or at least more straightforward. In the old days, when the coal miners glanced across and saw the canary keeled over, they knew they needed to get out or else! Getting out was the only way to stay alive. A similar, but less dramatic, theme exists for us today.

Stress and pressure surround us all the time. These elements of modern-day life are persistent, and like carbon monoxide, they are toxic. All of these little, and not-so-little, toxic stressors and pressures add up and we eventually become ill. Escaping from our toxic stressors is the only way to survive long enough to dig another day.

Here's the problem with those modern-day life toxins we face on a daily basis. We don't have canaries to warn us of these modern-day life dangers. Nor do we often give ourselves permission to get away when we start to feel unwell.

Again, our perceptions are different when it comes to physical injuries. We perceive those injuries with full clarity. If you sprain your ankle while running, the next day your ankle will be red, swollen, and painful. Your ankle will scream to you, "Don't run on me! I need time to heal." In this example, the pain is the canary; it's the signal to lay off.

No one runs on a sprained ankle. But what happens when the injury does not reside in the body? What happens when the pain can only be felt or experienced in our mind? In that sense, it's like everyone is mentally running on sprained ankles nowadays. Many of us (myself included) find ourselves leaning into the pain and suffering until we can arrive at our goal.

We tell ourselves to keep pushing through just until we cross some arbitrary finish line... just until the end of the year, just until I get that promotion, just until I can afford to buy a home, just until I can fit into those jeans that my dryer keeps shrinking on me. You can probably think of your own "just until" thoughts that run circles in your mind every day. More often than not, our diligence pays off and we do cross that finish line. We do accomplish our goals - at least some of them.

Unfortunately, this routine can be a trap. We're so used to the grind, that if we do manage to accomplish our goals, we just create a new finish line. Our minds instinctively cling to the idea that a challenge, once achieved, will deliver us that sense of ease or peace that we're aching for. But once we do achieve that goal, it's like we can't taste the victory. Unsatisfied, we move on to the next challenge.

As you may have experienced, this belief that accomplishing goals will result in a sense of peace and happiness doesn't often play out as planned. It's our own personal mythology. In a way, we make progress, but in another way, we end up losing so much more than we gain. We lose our sanity, our peace, our mental and physical health.

That's the trade-off. Suffer now, gain later. Dig deep today, enjoy tomorrow. This is a central reason why we perceive mental illness in a different way than we perceive physical illness. The things we do to push us towards a brighter future can easily be the same things that eat away at our internal reserves of energy and resilience.

Further, for some of us, the way we perceive emotional pain and mental suffering is that we just don't acknowledge it at all. The strategy, conscious or not, is to push it down. It's the old 'stuff it' technique. When our feelings are denied, ignored, or somehow rationalized away, we can make it through another day. Acknowledging it would then mean we are weak, or worse: a whiner. Complain too much, and there's a risk you may be a burden on others... which to some of us is the worst thing imaginable.

Our repression game is strong. That vomit-inducing anxiety? Must be a stomach bug. That constant distracted fogginess? I'm just tired. That sadness hollowing out your gut? Uh, never mind that, just go back to scrolling. We know it's there. It's real and it's bothersome. We just don't know what to do about it.

Due to this tendency to repress, we can easily find ourselves weighed down by symptoms of mental illness without being able to put words to the feelings. It's amazing how hard it sometimes is to explain to someone else the shape and feel of this thing we suffer through each day.

Imagine having a beloved pet with no name. Just think how hard it would be to baby talk your dog if you can't add extra, nonsensical syllables to their name when you're loving all up on them. How can you express what you're feeling? This is why, for many, just getting a diagnosis or name for their problem is such a relief in itself.

WHAT HAPPENED?!?

Mental illness often starts small and grows into something big. When it's big, it's also bewildering. Let's breakdown the timeline of its cancerous growth.

Some mental illnesses, ADHD for example, seem to strike at an early age without the help of life stressors. They can feel more genetic in nature. In these cases, there often was no classic life stressor or trauma. However, some other environmental factors could help bring it to the surface - things like nutrient deficiencies, altered gut bacteria, and environmental toxins. Other mental illness seems to be clearly related to the environment; this is the nature versus nurture debate.

Either way, it's important for us to start thinking about the environment we live in. We're surrounded by toxins, both physical and psychological. We can ask ourselves, "Is it me that's disordered or is it my environment?" In fact, this is how researchers are beginning to frame their understanding of PTSD (Post-Traumatic Stress Disorder). Some in the field are trying to turn our attention in PTSD away from the individual experiencing the symptoms and more towards the environment that pushed the individual to the point of experiencing PTSD symptoms.

Beyond the collection of environmental toxins, which we will cover later on in this book, there are those psychological stressors that we intuitively know are bad for us. These are the hurts, disappointments, conflicts, and struggles that mentally weigh on us.

Here's a quick rundown of how these psychological stressors may get us.

Some situation or interaction occurs and we get hurt. Whatever it is, it's powerful enough to gain access to our daily thoughts...and it won't leave. It's sticky. We're left with an unsettled feeling. This hurt playing on repeat is fertile ground for fear, anger, and sadness.

Without resolution to the situation, these uncomfortable feelings begin to grow. These hurts then color our future experiences with a certain shade of fear, anger, and self-doubt. A common storyline then emerges in our minds. Every experience seems to fit neatly into this exact storyline. The stories that follow sound like, "oh here I go again... why is this always happening to me... I'm so dumb... everyone hates me..." It can sound worse than that too. What began as hurt morphs into conscious thoughts and beliefs.

Once our thoughts join the party, things can go downhill quickly. Our feelings are often born irrational and have a way of making our thoughts continue on with the irrational. We go with those thoughts and believe them with 100% certainty. We slide down this slippery slope because our feelings are so powerful.

So here we are, stressing out, not thinking straight, maybe a touch delusional from all the intense fear, anger, and sadness. The stressed-out thoughts are constantly playing in the background, as it wears on our mind and our body. It saps our energy and steals our joy in life. The mental pain and suffering metastasize in our mind and spreads to our bodies. After a period of time living this way, we're so beaten down by negative thoughts that we, in subtle and not-so-subtle ways, stop taking good care of ourselves. This lack of self-care can recycle all that stress and hurt in our bodies and shoot it back up to our brains.

If you are feeling down, constantly worried, or lacking energy, could it be that you are mindlessly digging away in a cave full of carbon monoxide? Could it also be that you've ingested so much environmental toxicity that your brain is reeling? For many of us, the answer is both/and.

Your brain needs to be healthy and functioning at its best to be your partner in combatting negative thinking. Keeping fears in check and remaining clear-headed overall requires a brain that is not weighed down by all the toxicity described above. As we will see in the following chapters, breakdowns in brain functions can contribute to disturbed moods, anxiety, and all other forms of mental and emotional pain and suffering.

Mental illness symptoms are the canaries in the coal mine. To stay mentally and emotionally healthy (as best we can), we need to feed our brains the nutrients it needs and protect it from the flood of environmental toxins that it doesn't need. We also have to put negative thoughts in check on a daily basis.

BREAKING POINTS

Here's another possibility... like your ankle, your brain can send you warning signals. It could try to alert you in an effort to prevent you from reaching the brink.

First, it may scream out to you with thoughts like, "I'm overwhelmed! I need a break! Don't keep using and abusing me like this!" When it comes to sprained ankles we typically listen. When it comes to our brains and mental health, we're more likely to ignore the cries for help. If you ignore those initial warning signals, then your brain may up the ante in order to protect you from yourself.

What happens at that point where you can no longer stuff it and push through? A dense fog rolls in. Instead of isolated dark moments, the suffering may feel more constant. Your brain may be saying, "You didn't listen...but I won't be ignored, so take a seat." Ironically, this fog may be rolling in just in time to save you.

To be clear, I am not saying mental illness is our fault. Rather, just that life is hard. Our modern-day environment makes it that much harder. Defending our mental wellness against an onslaught of psychological and physical toxins in the environment is really difficult. It's not so easy to avoid smog, junk food, screen time, images of perfect people with perfect lives, and the reflections of our own blessed imperfections. Yet, taking action to defend ourselves is our responsibility.

It's hard. We can't always run and hide. We exist in the world, so we must get out there and try our best. Dysphoric moods, anxiety, or cognitive impairment may be the consequences of barreling through the pain of trying our best in this hypercompetitive world. Feeling mentally unwell may be the consequences of living in a mentally, emotionally, and physically toxic modern world.

CRUSHING IT?

Let's consider what it would mean if all of this were indeed true...for you. What if our emotions are signals being sent to us from us? What if these signals are trying to let us know that we are physically, nutritionally, mentally, emotionally, and even spiritually not okay?

If you are anemic due to not having enough iron, then you're very likely to be exhausted, and possibly depressed or anxious. Those symptoms are signals to go out there and get more iron. It likely works the same way for our mental and emotional distress.

What if sadness, isolation, panic, excessive worrying, and worse, are all just signals from the brain that we are not well? What if it is something in our food or environment that is messing around with our chemistry and causing us to react in certain ways? What if it's something related to our relationships, or our self-image that is producing our distress?

What if ignoring these signals just makes it worse? What if it's screaming out, trying to get us to stop and pay closer attention to what's going on in our environment and in our thoughts? What if our brains are trying to warn us so that we can start making some changes?

Who or what is to blame? That is not as important. What's more important is that we can see it. We need to foster an awareness of what's happening. We're better off entering difficult situations with our eyes wide open. Once our eyes are open, we can see what's happening and why. Once we know the "why", the "how" comes naturally.

Many of us, no doubt me included, at times choose not to listen. We like to dig deep, cut corners (in relation to our own well-being), and put our heads down as we keep slogging forward. Some of us may not have a choice. With ever-present responsibilities & pressures, it can be a requirement, not a choice, to push on through. But, it's a lot harder to see they "why" when our heads are down.

Ever heard the expressions, "a thorn in my side," or "I feel like my head is in a vice"? The point behind these analogies is that something external is causing pain for a person, but the source of that pain is not readily apparent. Imagine if you could not see the thorn or had no idea your head was lodged in a vice. The pain would be baffling. You'd feel it without any idea where it is coming from.

Unfortunately, this is a common scenario for people experiencing the pain of mental illness. The suffering is real...but the cause is unknown to us. Like the vice, it may be clearly visible to others, but we just can't see it. Either way, when we're hit with mental illness symptoms, finding the solution is never easy or quick. Once we look down and spot the thorn in our side, or grab a hand mirror and get a good look at the vice book-ending our head, we get an opportunity to fix the issue.

So how do we spot the problem? We have to listen to our thoughts and feelings, as well as our own body!

When we become more fully aware of our mental illness canaries and what they are trying to tell us, we're given the opportunity to change our environment and our thinking for the better. Taking steps to address the problem can usher in relief and allow you to recover.

But which steps need to be taken exactly? Where do we begin? There are some obvious, common life stressors that can push us toward this state of overwhelm...financial pressures, relationship conflicts, a crappy boss. All clearly toxic, none easily addressed.

Aside from the obvious ones, there are various life stressors that are unique to each of us. They belong to us, and may only be known by us. Not living up to the expectations we set for ourselves is a big one, as are issues with our identity and self-image. Many people struggle with unresolved past traumas. Our own personal reasons for our negative self-assessments are unique to each of us.

But harboring negativity is a universal feature of being human. Always has been. Now more than ever, there is a lot in the environment that can give us feedback on how we are not measuring up against our own idealized self-concept. That is a lot of opportunity to feel bad.

Modern-day life, with its uber-competitive social media-sphere, is our own high-tech version of the dusty, carbon monoxide filled coal mine. Remember, carbon monoxide is odorless. We can't sense it. The invasion occurs without warning. The harm infiltrates without our awareness. All we know is that we suddenly realize we don't feel well.

There seems to be added pressure in just standing and presenting yourself in front of others. How's my hair line? How's my waistline? How much do these shoes reflect how much money I make?

How can I get through today without letting on that I'm kinda messy inside? How can I say what I want to say without coming off as offensive?

Modern-day life has brought us many creature comforts. It also facilitated ingenuity, communication, and worldwide problem-solving. However, modern-day life is in many ways an enemy of mental health. There is a lot of added pressure these days - on top of the already difficult task of just being human. We are under constant threat of memes, mirrors, and measuring tapes.

Beyond the seemingly crushing social challenges of modern-day life, there is a collection of common environmental toxins (provided to us by modern-day life) that are really harmful to our bodies and brains. These toxins are familiar, but their effects on our mental health are not commonly known or understood.

Examples include processed foods that are exceptionally calorie-dense yet woefully nutrient deficient, absence of natural sunlight during our 9 to 5, spine altering body positioning (in cars, desks, couches), a barrage of assaults to quality sleep (light, electronics, entertainment, late night meals, all sorts of addiction), and relationships that are both hyperconnected & disconnected at the very same time. All of the above are perpetrated by modern-day life.

My hope for this book is to help bring awareness of the downsides of our convenient and comfortable, yet toxic modern-day lives. I want to shine a light on these insidious and pervasive environmental factors that impair our brains and irritate our minds. Currently, they are hiding in plain sight, but wreaking havoc on our insides. Like miners in a cloud of carbon monoxide, we aren't readily aware of the toxicity of these environmental factors, but we are surrounded by them.

The Mental Wellness Diet (TMWD) was put together with research from various fields, including mental health research, nutritional science, and even some anthropology.

The overarching principles are simple. We evolved on a certain kind of planet (green landscapes, clean air and water, only unprocessed whole foods, tight knit tribal communities, etc.), but we now find ourselves in a very different place with new and nearly invisible stressors. At the same time, the nutrients that helped our brains grow into the supercomputers they are today are now for the most part missing from our typical Western diet. We cannot go back to living as hunters and gatherers. But if somehow we could, that would be beneficial for our mental wellness in many ways.

By, taking advantage of the research we do have, we can use common sense and start making small tweaks here and there to improve our mental health. TMWD is about taking the best from the old and finding a way to make it fit within the new.

In opposition to the toxic environmental factors that promote mental illness, there is a collection of environmental factors that support and help optimize our mental health. These environmental factors are things like sunlight, sleep, nutrient dense food, movement, and connection with others.

A major theme in this book is awareness. It's the idea that we can pick out these environmental factors, both positive and negative, by looking back to traditional practices of our ancestors. This understanding shapes the guidance provided in the rest of the book. To be sure, scientific research is included in the text to verify that these recommendations are indeed restorative for our bodies and brains.

The next step is to put these behaviors and choices into daily practice so we can feel and function better. We also must identify the pressures to be who we feel we're supposed to be in modern-day life. And then, we need to decide to unburden ourselves of this pressure and step into being who we genuinely are.

The theory is that improving our relationship with our environment will help reduce the intensity of our mental illness symptoms overall. This includes setting better boundaries with environmental toxins and investing more quality time with those parts of the environment that do good things for us - exercise, sleep, sunlight, good food, play, supportive and accepting social connections. Hopefully, for future generations, we can incorporate these practices in our efforts not just to reduce mental illness symptoms, but effectively prevent them.

By going back to the basics and learning about what kind of environment in which we evolved, we can find a path to greater mental wellness.

WHAT THE BRAIN NEEDS

Sous Chef for the Brain

ROBOTS VERSUS ZOMBIES

The central idea behind this book is this: it's a good idea to give your brain the nutrition it needs, and limit the toxicity it doesn't need so you can feel and function at your best. Doing so will give you a better chance at resolving uncomfortable moods, reducing anxiety, and increasing focus and productivity.

To better understand the needs of the brain, let's take a detour into sci-fi. We can start by comparing the needs of three distinct complex systems – human beings, robots, and zombies. Now, we're not robots and we're not zombies either. But humans do share some things in common with each.

Robots are made of metal, grease, and circuit boards, but maintain no real prerogative of their own. They solely follow the instructions they are given. Similar to humans, robots have real needs. Robots need raw materials, fuel, and maintenance to function optimally. However, beyond all that impressive hardware, there's not much going on upstairs for robots... no self- awareness and no self-directed passions in life.

In this way, robots are pretty lame. They're incapable of originality, of creativity, of striving for more in life. But being that way saves them from the "monkey mind" that plagues humans. When you think about it, robots are masters of mindfulness. They can just perform their given tasks, and focus on just those tasks exceptionally well and move on to the next task. Plus, no matter what mean things you say to your electronic devices, they never take offense, and always show up for work the next day. In this way, being a robot has its advantages.

Zombies, on the other hand, don't have many needs; they do just fine lurking around for decades without any upkeep. It's unclear how they have the energy to linger on. They can foot drag their way across miles of obstacle heavy terrain with no real goal but to eat brains.

As impressive as their perseverance is, emotionally, zombies are a mess. Poor zombies moan and hiss, but they can't have themselves a good cry. They don't know how to make friends and are so one-dimensional with the whole "must eat humans" thing. Day in and day out, zombies just persist through the forest, totally parched, in search of their next meal. It's a never-ending, tortuous struggle.

Despite all that angst, you'd never catch a zombie working out their grief on a therapist's couch. They never stop to address the real issues, or try to make things better for themselves. Perhaps the clear-headed robots would make good therapists for these lost soul zombies.

Zombie: Ugggghhhhh

Robot: I can see you are upset. Please tell me more.

Zombie: Raaauugghhhh

Robot: That sounds difficult. How does that make you feel?

Zombie: Graahhhuugghhaaa

Robot: My algorithm tells me this is about your mother.

Zombie: Ghraammmhh

Anyways, it seems our bodies share more in common with robots than zombies. Focus on the right inputs, the body will respond as instructed. That's nice. But it may be that our modern-day lives are more aligned with the experience of zombies, which is not that nice. Modern-day life can feel like a never ending, meandering journey through the woods that leaves us feeling alone, unsatisfied, always hungry for more.

How many of us struggle to know if what we're after is the right thing? How many of us keep persisting despite uncertainty about whether we are even heading in the right direction? How many of us want to break free from the shackles of adult office worker-dom and enjoy life like we did when we were younger? How many of us feel disconnected from our purpose, from our relationships, from our reasons for doing things?

Humans are complex systems with diverse needs - both physical and psychological. We need to satisfy each of these needs to be able to function optimally. Like robots, we need the physical inputs – fuel, maintenance, and repair. But like zombies, we need to be more connected to our purpose and our own unique, inherently awesome, no-external-validation-needed identity.

Achieving peace of mind requires that we find ways to be driven and productive without the pain and suffering that so frequently comes with constantly seeking to be quicker, faster, stronger, better. It also requires a healthy, well-fed brain.

BRAIN DRAIN

As you'll discover in the following chapters, it's no wonder we are suffering so much. Our brains are starving with this Western pattern diet. Our brains are also overloaded in this modern-day lifestyle. When we don't give our bodies and brains what's needed, and we stress that system with constant psychological pressures, dysfunction will ensue. Similarly, our lifestyles are hungry for more meaning and healthy stimulation. We lost the genuine human connections that used to fill us up. We lost the time allotted to digesting life and making it mean something to us.

The following chapter will detail what we need to put on the dinner table to start feeling and functioning better. We have established thus far that consuming (and hopefully absorbing) a specific collection of dietary nutrients gives the brain what it needs to function at its best. This is common sense. But it's also backed up by research. Similarly, the solutions for our harmful modern-day lifestyle is outlined in chapter three – stress less about stuff that doesn't mean as much, stress more about the stuff that does.

Research exists that helps us understand what and how traditional cultures ate. Numerous fast food restaurants exist to provide examples of what we shouldn't eat. Many studies have examined the effects on human subjects when scientists artificially create a deficiency of a key nutrient. Related studies see what happens when key nutrients that are likely deficient are replenished with supplementation. And, there's incredibly dense and confusing research, filled with Latin sounding scientific terms and long, run-on sentences that clarify the mechanism of action for these key nutrients.

All of this research, as you can see with the hundreds of footnotes, accompanies the guidance provided throughout this book. It's there to back up the idea that the brain works better, and mental health symptoms tend to diminish, when we regularly consume foods with these key nutrients.

The final chapters contain diagrams to help explain exactly how all these key nutrients support the brain. These diagrams depict important processes in the brain (neurotransmitter activity, energy production, immune protection, balanced stimulation). They illustrate where the key nutrients highlighted in TMWD fit into those processes. These key nutrients all play specific roles in supporting our learning, memory, focus, and emotional regulation.

So get ready, things are about to pick up speed. Don't worry if you feel like all this science hits you like a ton of bricks. The take home point will remain the same. Take care of your brain. Feed it well. Don't overload it with unnecessary stress. Give it something big to work towards. Do that, and your brain will have the best chance at helping you to feel mentally well.

~ 3 ~

ANCIENT WISDOM – DIET

The Original Farm to Table

GRANDMA WAS RIGHT

My grandma knew best. How do I know?

First, she told me so. Second, she proved it with her resilience and longevity. She was born in Lebanon, and at age five emigrated to the United States through Ellis Island in New York. She survived the Great Depression. She raised seven children and put them all through college. She helped start the family's Middle Eastern restaurant and kept the back of the house humming for decades. Most impressive of all, she was upright and cooking in her kitchen well into her nineties.

She made a life for herself in the United States, but she kept many of her family's cultural traditions, especially the ones related to food. My grandma, we called her "Sitto" (Arabic word for grandmother), was actually my first exposure to the kind of traditional dietary practices highlighted in this book. Sitto loved to prepare fermented foods, organ meats, bitter vegetables, stews made from bone broth. To avoid being wasteful, she made use of the whole animal.

In growing up with less, she learned to make more out of what was available. Maybe it's no coincidence that she lived well into her nineties. Even at the end, she maintained her frugality. I remember visiting her at her final nursing home. In between blowing her nose with the stiff nursing home issued paper napkins, she would tear them up into quarters, just to avoid wasting.

Sitto also loved America. She loved funny TV commercials and would always repeat the tag lines. For the better part of 1991, she would greet me at her door with Ray Charles' Diet Pepsi™ tag line, "You got the right one, baby!".

Sitto was a big fan of pop culture, yet she never gave up her traditions. Thankfully so, a century after she first stepped foot in America, the wisdom she brought with her is now being validated by modern-day science. Turns out, when it came to the best diet for mental wellness, Sitto had the right one!

Food was my grandmother's way of expressing love. Every time I'd go visit, she would sit me down and make me eat huge bowls of food she had spent the better part of her days preparing. After I filled my belly, I'd start to struggle and try to tap out. Without fail, she'd swing by, pinch my cheek with her unforgiving fingers, and mumble something in Arabic as she passed by on her way back to the kitchen. I didn't always understand what she was saying, but I got the message - You better finish that bowl of food I just made for you.

If I fought my way through and finished the bowl, it was 50/50: either she'd slip me a twenty-dollar bill, or hand me another bowl full of food. Sitto knew there was some sort of magic in good food. To her, it was the most important gift she could give. Good, home-cooked food equaled good health. She was fond of saying, "your health is your wealth!".

My grandma was something else, but she wasn't alone in terms of her traditional diet. In examining traditional cultures across the globe, we can find many similarities. Despite traditional diets being frugal and not very cutting edge, they are amazing for optimizing brain function.

Without the benefit of scientific research, traditional cultures have gravitated towards fermentation, eating the whole animal, prioritizing foods from the oceans, and eating a variety of bitter and flavorful plants. The alternative to traditional diets is the 'better living through science' approach promoted by the massive commercial interests in our food and health industries.

It was modern-day corporations that invented the kinds of foods – processed grains, vegetable oils, refined sugars, and food additives – that took us backwards in terms of the health of our brains and bodies. Scientists in a lab created these artificial ingredients, not mother nature. Loading up processed and packaged foods with artificial ingredients allow them to stay on shelves longer. This led to greater corporate profits, but also a greater amount of people with chronic physical and mental illnesses. Processed and artificial foods do not give our brains what they need. Rather, these ingredients and means of processing are often toxic to our bodies and brains.

The only thing my grandma let us add to our food was salt and lemon juice. And, we had to wait to eat. In her home, food was not fast. It was cherished. None of our modern-day foods or conventions can be credited to traditional cultures. Nor do modern-day foods carry the same emotional attachment that my grandma applied to her cooking.

Looking back, I'm glad I didn't argue (I wouldn't have had the courage to do so anyways). She got a lot right. As more and more research on these traditional foods and practices continues to emerge, it becomes increasingly clear exactly how consuming them helps, avoiding them hurts, and replacing them with modern-day processed food is a mistake.

TMWD was built around key foods that offer the exact nutrients the brain needs to function at its best. What's in these foods is what you want in your brain and body. These foods are not new; they're ancient.

ANCIENT FOODS:

Ancient foods, as a term in this book, refers to some of the popular and many of the less popular parts of animals, a vast array of edible plants, and ways of preparing foods that have been nearly lost in modern society. These foods and practices were all commonplace in traditional cultures, but currently hold a limited presence in our modern-day diet.

Modern-day life more often features a Western pattern diet, commonly known as the standard American diet. The Western pattern diet is generally devoid of nutrients, but full of calories and convenience. It reflects a society that is on the go. Further, it prioritizes easy access and hyper-palatability (intense and likely addicting flavors) over health, nutrition, and giving the brain what it needs to thrive.

The Western pattern diet does include some foods found in the TMWD, such as red meat, butter, dairy, and potatoes. Yet, also on the list are many of the foods TMWD rejects. These include processed meats, processed grains, industrial seed oils (vegetable oils from canola, soy, corn, among others), sugary snacks and drinks, and mutant compounds like high fructose corn syrup.

Similar to the fast-food diet described above, we live a fast-paced, stress inducing, uber-competitive, sleep-when-you're-dead modern-day lifestyle. As you may have guessed, the opposite lifestyle is likely to welcome more wellness into our lives.

In Chapter 3, we will dive into the lifestyle practices that complement the TMWD foods. These lifestyle practices stimulate and heal our brains. They offer a counterbalance to the modern-day stressors that inundate our brains on a daily basis.

Diet and lifestyle seem like two totally separate topics, one you eat, the other you do. But in reality, they fold onto one another: the better you eat, the better you feel and perform. The more you focus on improving your habits, the better you tend to eat. Think about when you crave sweets. Is it when you are with friends and having a ton of fun? Or do you more often lean towards the freezer and "reward" yourself with a pint of ice cream after a hellish day?

The logic here is that the body and brain need certain nutrients to function optimally. The opposite is also true, our brains function better when some foods are absent (think sugar, trans fats, pesticide residues, and artificial additives). When our brain is flush with the nutrients it needs for neurotransmitter function, energy production, waste removal, neuronal communication, and balanced immune function, then our brain functions better. As a result, we feel and perform better.

For example, if our brains are not functioning at top speed, our performance at work will likely suffer. Often our only answer to this problem is to dedicate more time to work. If we can't get done what we need to in a day (either at work or at home), we tend to steal time from ourselves in one way or another later on. We skip the gym, pass on dinner with friends, collapse on the couch after a long day. Being more efficient allows us to stop and let work go when the workday is done – that allows more time to spend on ourselves and our loved ones.

We need to give our brain what it requires to function optimally so we can leave our workday feeling accomplished, content, and at ease. A better functioning brain allows us to be more efficient. The opposite is also true – brain fog ruins everything. Imagine finishing your day feeling accomplished. Driving home, starting dinner, heading to the gym all feel so much better when we aren't weighed down by thoughts about how we could have done, should have done, or still need to do.

Staying sharp limits that ever-burning fear inside us that we are not doing enough, or worse, the fear that others will catch on to our inefficiency – inefficiency due to poor focus, sunken moods, or terribly distracting anxiety. Time lost to brain fog, anxiety, and depressed moods is just health and wellness lost to ourselves. What we eat matters.

Humans have been successfully following these ancient food diets and practices for centuries. Now these foods and practices are about to trend hard. These foods (organ meats, bone broths, shellfish, fermented foods, among others) and practices (sunlight, exercise, community, relaxation, meaning and purpose, among others) are thankfully gaining momentum.

The nutrients plentiful in TMWD, but lacking in the Western pattern diet, are now receiving more media attention. Even more exciting, these nutrients and practices are finding support in current scientific research for their role in supporting brain health and emotional wellbeing.

To be sure that myself and my grandma are totally legit, we can look to five criteria to judge whether or not a specific key nutrient - and by extension the ancient foods overflowing with this particular key nutrient - should be accepted or rejected in TMWD.

All of the ancient foods (organ meats, fish and shellfish, connective tissue foods, fermented foods, nuts and seeds, and fruits and veggies) highlighted in TMWD earned their place on the list of high priority because they met these five important criteria.

FIVE CRITERIA:
1. Scientific research has identified a mechanism for how this key nutrient (found in high concentrations in ancient foods) improves brain health and function.
2. Scientific research demonstrates that depleting this key nutrient (found in high concentrations in ancient foods) is associated with greater mental illness symptoms.
3. Scientific research demonstrates that replenishing this key nutrient (found in high concentrations in ancient foods) is associated with improvements in mental health.
4. Traditional cultures valued and incorporated these ancient foods.

5. Standard American or Western pattern diets are lacking in these ancient foods, and by extension, the key nutrients on which the brain thrives.

THE UNUSUAL SUSPECTS:

The following list of ancient foods all share a unique quality: they are all very nutrient dense. Foods with higher nutrient density is what TMWD is after.

Nutrient density is the ratio of beneficial nutrients to calories in a given food. This means that for every bite of TMWD food you consume, you will take in significantly more key nutrients than you would from a bite of food from the Western pattern diet.

ORGAN MEATS

When it comes to nutrient density, the edible meats that come from organs like liver, kidney, heart, and others are a cut above.[17-18]

Let's think about it. Animals (humans alike) store nutrients in organs because those nutrients are needed, in ample supply and at the ready, to support the function of those vital organs. Organs are like your pantry or refrigerator. If you're starving, or find yourself needing a snack, you head straight there to quickly grab what you need.

Organ meats are some of the most nutrient dense foods on the planet because they need to be. Their jobs are so important and time sensitive, they need a ready supply of nutrients. Given that our brain is also an organ, it makes sense that it likes to soak up and utilize as many nutrients as possible.

Many of these nutrients serve as catalysts. They increase the rate of activity of enzymes, which in turn speed up metabolic processes in the body. If nutrients are in short supply, the enzymes will not be able to keep up with the demands of the body. The brain also needs fast and responsive metabolism to help us effectively deal with life.

Without key nutrients keeping the metabolic activity humming along, our brains will not be as responsive. Our brain works best when it is running on all cylinders. If you want that, then look to organ meats for support. What's the simplest and most efficient way to make sure your brain has stores of nutrients that it needs? Eat organ meats, regularly.

Recommendation

At least once, try cooking some liver. It's cheap, and relatively easy to make. The taste will not be for everyone. I resisted my mom's version when I was a kid. The opportunity was given, but I blew it. Don't be like young me, give it a try. Below is my mother's recipe, which is my go-to today.

Liver can be obtained at any quality grocery store. The meat department typically sells beef or chicken livers at the counter - and it's usually pretty cheap! Preparing it is easy: just rinse and pat dry. Coat the liver pieces with a ton of seasonings - salt, pepper, garlic powder, onion powder, thyme, cumin. Coating the entire surface of the liver pieces tends to improve the sear, which will improve the taste.

Next, brown some bacon in a skillet on medium. My mom swears by bacon grease as a flavor enhancer. Once the bacon is browned and the bacon grease is pooling, turn the stove down to medium-low and toss in the liver. Keep a close eye on the liver, making sure that the sides are browned, but flip soon enough so that the middle of the liver pieces remain a little red/pink. Beyond 2-3 minutes on each side is too long. Cooking to the point of brown all the way through will change the taste and texture for the worse.

If you're not ready for all that, another way is to chop up raw liver into bits and mix it in with ground beef. Cook the mixture on medium in a skillet on the stove. Aim for just browned all the way through for both the liver and ground beef. To accompany the mean, I wait until I have too many veggies in the fridge. Instead of tossing them out, I'll use this savory concoction to turn them into vehicles of flavor. Make sure you start with a skillet that is big enough for everything.

Once browned, I take off the heat and set aside. Next, I heat up some olive oil in a skillet on the stove and toss in whatever vegetables I have on hand. When the veggies are soft, I add the meat mixture, then cover all of it with a jar of tomato sauce and add whatever spices seem like a good fit.

This smorgasbord of a creation saves me from having to toss out vegetables (the ones I promised myself at the grocery store that I would definitely use, but never did) and covers up the intense flavor of the liver at the same time.

Finally, if neither of these options work for you, there are liver supplements available. Look for reputable brands of desiccated (dried and chopped up) versions of liver that can be taken in capsules. This might feel like cheating, but it works just as well, and no one is judging.

CONNECTIVE TISSUES

I know we just finished talking about organ meats but bear with me. We don't have to go all feral & eat live animals to enjoy the benefits of connective tissue foods. Our ancestors knew that connective tissues— bones, skin, tendons, ligaments, cartilage, and fascia— are all highly nutrient dense parts of the animal that should be consumed for optimal health and wellness. They also knew their teeth weren't sharp enough to easily consume these parts of the animals raw. So, they got creative and came up with ways to consume connective tissues without the jaw ache.

Various cultures took advantage of hot water to make broths and stocks out of bones and other parts of the animal. With this approach, the good parts leach out of the bones and connective tissues into the water. The remaining liquid is much easier to take down compared to the bones and connective tissues.

Connective tissues contain certain nutrients that are truly diffi-cult to find elsewhere. Primarily, they offer an amino acid profile that compliments the amino acid profile of muscle meat, which most of us are eating all the time.

As you'll see below, animal meat (cuts of muscle) is on the list of important foods. For example, muscle meat provides higher amounts of methionine, which is vital for brain function and re-building our body.[18-19] Connective tissues deliver higher amounts of glycine, an amino acid central for a number of different functions in the brain and body.[18,20] One amino acid is not more important than the other. We need both working in synergy. In the Western pat-tern diet, glycine is typically lacking.

Recommendation:

You don't need to be on a trapped-in-the-wilderness reality TV show to figure out how to get more connective tissues in your diet. A simple first step is to just start by cooking meats that still have the bone in. Also, invest time into learning how to make bone broth – from real bones. Plenty of good recipes exist online, and you'll find an easy slow cooker version in the recipe section below.

Last, if those steps are not as doable just yet, consider supple-menting with collagen peptide powder. There are a few trustwor-thy companies out there that make great powders that mix easily into hot or cold liquids.

If the is taste hard to handle, try this:

Heat water in a tea kettle. Grab a pint glass. Toss in two scoops of collagen peptides, and two tea bags (rooibos teas is great for the brain). Add the hot water and stir until all the collagen has dis-solved. Sip on this for breakfast and note how you feel throughout the day. Or, down it at night and see if it improves your sleep.

SHELLFISH

When it comes to vitamin and mineral content, oysters, mussels, clams, shrimp, scallops, and lobster blow all other foods out of the water.[18,21] Shellfish are some of the most ancient living species still around today. Maybe it's the hard shells that help keep all those nutrients inside that enhanced their survival. Maybe they know something we don't when it comes to storing up brain saving nutrients. We could ask them their secret, or we can just eat them. These little nutritional powerhouses are chock-full of the vitamins and minerals that keep the gears grinding in our brains. They are also provide some of the harder-to-find vitamins and minerals that the brain craves, like B12, zinc, and copper.

Recommendation:

If you think about it, whether you're going out to dinner or grilling at home, it's usually chicken or beef. Am I right? Preparing shellfish at home is more challenging to master. Undercooking is always a fear, overcooking forever a frustration. Lucky for us, many restaurants offer shellfish dishes that have been perfected over time. You always have to be careful with sourcing of shellfish, but most good restaurants typically get it right. Why not take advantage of a professional's cooking (and cleaning up after), and order up the mussels, clams, scallops, or even oysters next time you are out to eat?

If the scent or taste of seafood is not for you, there is a solution. Similar to how we can get around the not-for-everyone flavors of organ meats, we can look to supplements. A few reputable supplement companies make capsules filled with desiccated (dried and chopped up) mussel or oyster meat. If we want to have something positive to say about modern life, I guess it would be making these ancient foods easier to take in through supplement form.

If I had to pick a top three of foods that help the brain, organ meats, connective tissues, and shellfish would be them. I wouldn't recommend eating only these three foods. Nor would I say that you need to consume them three times a day, every day (the same goes for the next ancient food, animal meats). I would say, however, that failing to consume them regularly may limit your optimal state of mental wellness.

Unfortunately, most of us did not grow up eating these kinds of foods on a regular basis. Our taste buds did not have the chance to develop an appreciation for their strong flavors and aromas. It may be too late to learn to love these foods, but give it a try and see!

ANIMAL MEAT

In recent years, there's been a lot of controversy surrounding the health benefits, risks, and ethics of consuming meat. Obviously, TMWD does not fit with the beliefs and practices of vegetarianism or veganism. In a way, I wish it were different. I feel that those who promote awareness of animal rights have very valid points - particularly when it comes to the treatment of livestock and the abuse of our environment.

However, as a species, I believe our optimal health depends on us consuming animals. For some, it may be impossible to reconcile the idea of harming animals with our own health needs. Yet, plenty of research points to the vital importance of animal foods for the historical development of the human brain.[22-23]

On a practical note, animal meats provide some key nutrients that plant foods do not – or at least not in sufficient amounts. The same nutrients that are critical for brain function are also the ones we find in animal meat. They include the highly form of absorbable iron,[17] as well as zinc,[24] copper,[24] vitamin B12,[17,25] methionine and glycine,[17] among others.

Like organ meats, muscle meats carry a decent amount of nutrients the brain needs for optimal functioning. The key nutrients mentioned above are critical for balanced and responsive neurotransmitter activity.

You've probably heard the phrase "grass-fed" from advertisements or seen it on packaging at the grocery store. It may sound like a marketing gimmick, but there are some clear benefits to eating animals that have grazed on grasses or pastures - rather than ones fed processed grains like corn, soy, or wheat. Animals that graze on grasses will produce a healthier balance of polyunsaturated fatty acids in their muscles and organs.[26] As mentioned above, iron, zinc, copper and vitamin B12 are all found in high concentrations in red meat. These nutrients are critical for neurotransmitter activity and overall brain function. They are also, by comparison, less available in plant foods - especially from processed grains like corn, soy, or wheat.

If you have heard the warnings about the dangers of red meat, you may be hesitant. Thankfully, recent research took a second look and debunked this misguided warning.[27]

Recommendation:

Proceed as you did 15 years ago, before all the anti-meat hysteria. Fire up some steaks on the grill. Roast that 8-pound chicken. Sear a pork loin, and pop it in the oven to finish it off. You know what to do. Tell your vegan friends, "I love you, and I'm sorry that I'm just not that sorry. I love tasty meat!" Then go cook that meat with your head held high! Just make sure to prioritize "grass-fed" and "pasture-raised" when and where you can.

FERMENTED FOODS

Most traditional cultures have their own classic versions of fermented food. Often used as a garnish, traditional cultures knew enough to incorporate fermented foods like kimchi, sauerkraut, kefir, kombucha, yogurt, miso, tempeh, and of course pickles into their regular diets.

The most basic fermentation process involves picking plants from the soil and allowing them to soak in water and salt. When the plants are uprooted, they retain the bacteria from the soil and their own parts. In the brine of salt and water, the lactic acid bacteria are able to multiply over time. This produces a bitter but flavorful bacteria-rich treat.[28]

Since the invention of antibiotics, our modern society had tended to consider all types of bacteria as without-a-doubt, across-the-board bad for us. With new information coming down the nutritional science pipeline, attitudes are changing. Now people are lining up to ingest probiotic bacteria in the form of pills, powders, and fizzy drinks.

Not all the claims are fully established at this point, but there is a good amount of science backing up many of the health claims. Probiotics are supplements made up of "good bacteria" that in one way or another have proven, in clinical human trials, to improve one health condition or another.

When it comes to brain health, certain bacteria, common in fermented foods, have been found in studies to interact with our nervous, digestive, and immune systems in helpful ways. These effects on our bodies have also demonstrated benefit for our brains.[29]

In relation to our mental wellness, the general effect of probiotics is that they calm the nervous system.[30-32] Maybe our ancestors understood the brain benefits of fermented foods, or maybe they were just trying to find a way preserve their food supply to last through the winter. Who knows?

Whatever the case, we are the beneficiaries of so many different kinds of fermented foods from all over the world. What could be more fun than sampling the intense fermented flavors from various cultures? Experiment and see what you like. Your brain, in addition to your taste buds, may thank you.

Recommendation:

A perfect way to introduce fermented foods is to think of them as condiments. Add a little spicy kimchi to your eggs in the morning. Cozy up some sauerkraut next to your sausage and peppers. Try yogurt and kombucha as tide-me-overs in between meals. If you're looking for a snack with a satisfying crunch, try pickles.

Some brands will be better than others. The majority of fermented foods sold in jars and other containers will have been pasteurized to kill all the bacteria, then a few probiotic strains are tossed back in. There are some way better options. When choosing a brand, dig a little deeper. See what you can find about the methods of production. Unless you're sensitive due to immune issues, look for labels that note "unpasteurized", "raw", or "live cultures."

Can't stand the texture or taste of fermented foods? One option is to start with just a tiny bit and build up your palate's preference. The other option is probiotic capsules. Again, quality varies. Doing a little research will help. Any probiotic worth it's price tag will offer between 100 million and 10 billion colony forming units (CFU) per dose. Also, make sure part of the label speaks to "quality assurance" practices that the manufacturer follows.

In addition to probiotics, prebiotics are another kind of supplement that increases the population and benefits of good bacteria in the gut. Thus, prebiotics are just as important, if not more important, than probiotics. They provide sustenance for your resident gut bacteria. Feed your good gut bacteria, and they will return the favor by boosting your mood and brain function. Think of the variety of plant – fruits and vegetables – that are likely already a part of your diet. You don't need to go bananas with fermented foods and fermentable prebiotic fiber to satisfy your brain's needs. But, consuming plants with every meal is a great strategy to help your inner gut bacteria help you.

~ 4 ~

ANCIENT WISDOM- LIFESTYLE

Untraditional Traditions

Sunlight:

You're likely aware that sunlight is the catalyst for the creation of Vitamin D in our bodies. Specifically, UVB radiation activates the pro-hormone of Vitamin D and converts it into the useable form Vitamin D in our body.[33] Vitamin D then goes on to regulate our immune system,[34-36] support the growth and repair of neurons,[37-38] and play a part in the production of neurotransmitters in our brains – including serotonin.[39-40] Seeing that 80% of our Vitamin D stores come from sun exposure, sunlight is Vitamin D's wingman.[41]

Beyond providing vitamin D, sunlight sends some important signals to the body and brain. Exposure to the sun's rays triggers the release of nitric oxide, which then supports the heart, lungs, and blood vessels.[42]

Sunlight is a powerful regulator of our daily rhythms as well. These rhythms follow the sun's path through the day.[43-44] Our circadian rhythm is an internal biological clock that orchestrates all the chemical activity swishing around in our brain and body throughout the day. It is the reason why we are up and alert during the day and get tired and sleepy at night. Our circadian rhythm depends on the different types of sunlight exposure we experience throughout the day.

Morning light alerts us to the need to move our bodies and release energy. The red hue of sunset preferentially converts serotonin to melatonin to help orchestrate the onset of sleep.[45] The absence of sunlight, also known as darkness, allows our bodies to fall deeper into sleep and engage in restorative processes.[46] Morning sunlight exposure anchors your circadian rhythms to a pattern of being awake and moving during the day and asleep and still at night.

Further, greater light exposure during the morning and midday preps us to respond better to darkness as a cue for falling asleep.[47] Following a daily activity pattern that is aligned with the sun's rise, peak, and setting is really important to many biological rhythms inside your body and brain.

Recommendation:

Get outside and let your body see the sun for at least 15-30 minutes per day. In the morning or first part of the day is best, as light exposure in the beginning of the day helps to reset our 24-hour circadian rhythm.

No need to splay out angled perfectly toward the sun, as we do in our search for the perfect tan. Just being outside, while sunlight is making contact with your skin and the retinas of your eyes, will send powerful signals to help regulate many important systems in our bodies and brains.

Movement:

Movement is vital to brain function in so many ways. To make any movement, we must mentally plan our actions before we initiate them. Most movements are so routine that we aren't aware of the mental pre-planning that's going on. But movement gives us a chance to learn how to anticipate and respond. That's great 'exercise' for our brains.

In this way, movement can also help us wriggle free from destructive emotions.[48-49]Movement not only provides a distraction from intense emotions, it also helps us to feel more confident in our ability to meet challenges, overcome obstacles, and master our problems.

On a more spiritual and emotional level, movement changes our perspective. Movement creates a wedge between us and the obstacles that worry or challenge us. Instead of being paralyzed by our fears, consumed by our emotions, and swallowed up by our stress, we can move out of those spaces and into a state of mastery and control through exercise and movement.

What's the #1 piece of advice you'll hear after a tough break up? Survey says... go for a run! It makes intuitive sense that we need to shake off what is pulling us down through movement and exercise.

On the physiological level, exercise is good for our brains because it pumps more oxygen upstairs.[50-51] That oxygen, combined with a fuel source like glucose, then

gives our neurons the energy they need to function optimally. At the same time, exercise increases the removal of wastes, which again serves to help our brain function at its best.[52]

Beyond that, newer research has discovered other mechanisms whereby exercise boosts brain function and mood. For example, brain-derived neurotrophic factor (BDNF) is a brain chemical that acts like a fertilizer for neurons, which enhances learning and mood.[53-54] Exercise intensely enough and BDNF will spike in the brain.[55-56] Generally, the more BDNF you have circulating, the better your brain function and mood will be.[57-58]

Recommendation:

Do some strength training, do a little cardio, and don't forget to move your body for fun. Strength training builds mitochondria,[59-60] which provides us a reserve of easily accessible energy when we need it. This is important as we go through life and experience stressors and demands on our energy system.[61] Having that buffer puts less pressure on our blood sugar regulation mechanisms,[62] helps reduce oxidative stress[63-65] and inflammation,[65-66] and provides needed energy for neurons to continue to hum along throughout the day.[67-68]

When you're trying to lose weight, cardio alone can be hit or miss. But if you want to feel instantaneously better mentally and emotionally, cardio is king. Variation in intensity helps with creating the stimulus for BDNF surges and other healthy chemical responses in your body. For general boost in mood, reduction of anxiety, and sharpening of cognition, however, most studies reveal that steady state cardio for 20 minutes or longer will do the trick.[69-70] Going 40 to 60 minutes increases the benefits.[71-72]

If you're looking for something shorter in duration or more exciting, try intervals. Whatever the rhythmic movement (running, cycling, swimming), warm up and then go for 6-8 rounds of 15 seconds on, 45 seconds off. That will give your brain and body the internal chemical change that will help tame emotional distress.

Stress Management:

STRESS IS GOOD, BUT NOT TOO MUCH

You've probably heard that not all stress is bad stress. Some stress is good for us. It's actually true. Experiencing stress is the definition of being alive. Stress can push us to do or handle more than we ever thought we could. But, if the stress we face is too much, if it exceeds our ability to cope, the mental illness symptoms can result.

But there's a saying in medicine: "The dose makes the poison." Too much stress —unrelenting, insurmountable, overwhelming stress— eats away at our reserves of patience, energy, and inner strength. When that resilience is lost, we suffer mental and emotional pain.[73]

Yet, stress is only one side of the equation. The other side is our genes and our physical health. The equation looks like this: Stress X Genetic Predisposition = Mental Illness.

Among the many gifts our parents pass down to us, genetic predisposition for health and disease is the gift that keeps on giving. We are born with a certain likelihood, or risk, that mental illness will strike. Stress is the factor that activates your genetic predisposition and pushes you over the edge into mental illness.

This is why we do better when we pay attention to what's happening in our lives and take steps to lessen our overall stress. It's an essential.

LET'S GET PHYSICAL

Ever wonder what's going on in the body during stress? We've all heard that stress can give us ulcers and raise our blood pressure. But, how exactly? The general answer is that emotional or psychological stress breeds oxidative stress[74-76] and inflammation[77] in the body.

Errrrr.. say what? Inflammation and oxidative stress are scientific terms for normal destructive processes in the body. The destruction is a good thing - in measured doses. We need inflammation to tear down aging cells and clear our foreign substances. When there's too much inflammation going on, we call that... inflammation. In technical terms, it's chronic, low grade, systemic inflammation. Or, inflammation, for short.

Chronic means the inflammation has been going on for too long. Low-grade means there's not a lot of inflammation, but more than is needed at that time. Systemic means all over the body, not just in the one spot you need it – so everywhere suffers unnecessarily.

Oxidation is like car exhaust. It is a natural byproduct of things getting converted from one thing into another thing in the body. When that happens (too much oxidation happening) the body tissues get worn down or destroyed. Excess oxidation can then lead to excess inflammation, and vice versa. Inflammation and oxidative stress are normal biological activities. At lower levels, they're needed to regenerate the body. At excessive levels, they harm the body and brain.

What happens when our bodies are awash with oxidative stress and inflammation? We can experience depressed moods,[78-79] excessive anxiety,[80] fatigue,[81] weight gain,[82] and brain fog,[83] to name a few. Living with constant stress is literally like playing with fire (in the figurative sense of literally, but like literally).

OPTIONS COME STANDARD

Stress is a part of life, always has been. However, the stress we face today is wholly different than the stress our living elders, or distant ancestors faced. Compared to our ancestors, the stress we face is way worse in a couple of ways. The stress that confronts us nowadays is not just any stress. It's chronic stress.

It's easier to stay alive these days. But, in a sense, it's actually harder to feel alive. Nowadays, we often can't really relax because there is so much coming at us. So many decisions to be made, so many options to be considered, so many associated fears and angst. With so much information to process, we can get overwhelmed. Once overwhelmed, we struggle to make decisions. If we can't decide, we don't act. If we don't act, then things go south. Then we can start to feel like our personal inadequacies are to blame, which just worsens our stress.

Before, the stress was about trying to survive. Hunt, eat, avoid being eaten, procreate, and then relax in the tall grass. Nowadays, with so many options for what we can become or what we can make of ourselves, it's like we're stuck in a metaphorical cereal aisle with a blank shopping list in our hand that reads, "Make sure you pick the right one!" at the top. It's a set up. Endless choices, only one right answer. Go. The multitude of options, paired with the sense that any choice could be a mistake, creates an immense amount of stress and pressure.

Think of the non-violent threats that exist in the modern-day workplace. Big bureaucratic organizations are the new torture dungeons of modern-day life, rampant with passive aggressive coworkers, gaslighting managers, and the ever-present glass ceiling. Many people head home from a long day of work wondering if they truly are as 'in need of improvement' as their employer makes it seem.

Food is much easier to get. But it's the Frankenfoods that come in shiny packages, irritate your gut, and leave you feeling full for minutes then devastatingly ravenous thereafter. We wonder, "Should I eat more?... Am I still hungry?"

It is so much easier to shop for stuff these days, as it is to get the feeling of immediate regret for spending money you don't really have. "Do I really need this? I feel like I do. But I always say that, then regret it. Whatever, just click the big blue buy now button."

There is no relief from these modern-day chronic stressors; they're all around us, all the time. So many questions, so few answers. Without realizing it, we are drowning in stress and pressure.

Modern-day life presents us with more choices than we could ever make. Our brains have not yet caught up to all this nuanced opportunity for making the wrong decision. Surviving another winter used to be the goal. Now the goal is living your best life. But society has normalized this chaos. When exponential options are the norm, we just put our heads down and pretend like we got this.

ACUTE VERSUS CHRONIC

Scientific research on stress originated in the laboratory of the great Han Selye.[84] His paradigm shifting research involved poking rats with needles and sometimes injecting them with adrenaline. Those poor rats endured a lot in the pursuit of scientific advancement. And, they were definitely stressed out to the max from all that poking and prodding.

This original research on stress gave us the idea that stress was bad for us, which is no surprise. It didn't end well for the rats. But there is an important difference between the kind of stress these rats experienced in the lab and the types of stress that real human beings face in the world on a daily basis.

Although we don't have those same acute stressors, we sure do experience acute stress. Traffic jams, financial strains, arguments with loved ones, professional failures, not knowing which option to select, and all kinds of modern-day stressors can still get us going.

One key difference with our stressors now is that they are often intangible. They are less of the physical world (predators, famine, cold), more psychological in nature (perceived inadequacy, contempt, guilt, shame). Our psychological stressors have so much more territory to invade in our minds because they are intangible, invisible, and often never spoken of.

Another difference with our stressors today is that they tend to come at us all at once, from multiple angles, and to go unresolved for longer periods of time. As society progressed, the landscape of our lives changed. We moved indoors. We learned how to cook and how to store food for later. We invented accountants, lawyers, and food delivery services. The result... less physical challenges, greater perceived stress, more chronic inflammation, worse sleep, and rollercoaster blood sugar levels. And, the stress turned chronic... no more breaks in between.

The take home point is that the human brain was designed to handle and adapt to acute stress, not chronic, unrelenting stress.[85-86] By definition, acute stress happens, and then it stops. There's some time to recover before the next bout.

Acute stress can make us stronger only because at some point it stops. Once the acute stressor ceases, the body and mind can then get to work healing, recovering, and adapting in ways that help you come back stronger. This is how stress builds resilience.

Chronic stress doesn't stop long enough for the pendulum to swing back in the other direction. It doesn't allow us as much opportunity to develop resilience. The type of chronic stressors we face constantly in modern-day life are less extreme, but it adds up over time. The weight of all that accumulated stress harms our bodies and brains in subtle, insidious ways.

Chronic psychological stress can be destructive not only physically, but mentally and emotionally as well.[87-88] It's important to reiterate that emotional or psychological stress breeds oxidative stress[74-76] and inflammation[77] in the body.

What symptoms can we expect when our bodies are awash with oxidative stress and inflammation again? We can experience depressed moods,[78-79] excessive anxiety,[80] fatigue,[81] weight gain,[82] and brain fog[83] to name a few.

In sum, acute stress, which comes and goes, is potentially more painful, but far less damaging in the long run when compared to chronic stress. Acute we can handle. Chronic takes us down.

How is it that in modern-day life, with so many advancements in science, technology, and civility, we are actually moving backwards in terms of stress management? Our never-ending quest for better, quicker, stronger has a lot to do with it.

OLD VERSUS NEW

Fast forward from caveman days to the glory days of the 1970s and 1980s. This is when it became that much easier (for most in society) to obtain our basic survival needs. Hence, they dubbed the 1970s the "me generation", and the 1980s the "decade of greed."

Food for thought: without the threat of not making it to the end of day (due to predators, floods, famine, frigid weather, or rival tribes), we turned our attention in modern day life toward bettering ourselves.

This included finding ways to get ahead, to make more money, to save time, to increase our efficiency, to look better physically, etc. It was like we couldn't give up our addiction to stress. Things were easier, but we got creative and found ways to make it harder again. Once life was much less stressful, we found new things to stress over. One of the things we decided to stress over was the challenge of finding the best way to manage our stress.

In the old days, when tigers, or our enemies, were on the prowl, our ingrained fear and anxiety were protective. Keeping alert, aware, and ready for action was an inner tension that was worth the emotional distress. Fear of danger kept us away from danger. Fear of starvation kept the hunter-gatherers on the move and the early farmers vigilant over their crops during the night watch.

Along the way, some genius invented a world changing apparatus called a fence. We fenced in our crops, animals, and loved ones. Another early mental giant came up with the concept of... the shed. Then, we were able to store our crops and make it last through the winter. After that, we were able to stay put in one place, and just focus on living. It was finally easier.

These early civilizations had healthy food, protection from invaders, and a well-connected community. Maybe not so strange that these key elements are what many health gurus today are asking us to focus on: exposure to the sun, movement and exercise, sound sleep, social connections, and community.

Unfortunately, we humans didn't stop there. We kept trying to make things better, faster, stronger, quicker, more efficient, and easier. We progressed, but at what cost?

Progress is a good thing. One of the key lifestyle recommendations in this book is to find meaning and purpose in life. Finding purpose in life inevitably ends up in progress being made. Most people truly connected to their purpose in life will be working diligently towards improving the life of at least one other person, if not the entire world.

However, the drive towards self-improvement can be a double-edged sword. What helps us live easier, obtain more, and be better can also be our downfall. What do we give up in exchange for an easier time in life? If we shortcut the process, we miss out. Sometimes, we miss out on finding out who we are. We miss out on the beauty of seeing ourselves persevere through difficulty, disappointment, and despair. If we're struggling, then maybe that's a sign we're doing something right. However, that's not the first conclusion many of us jump to.

Because things can be so easy nowadays, and because society has made so much progress, it has become harder to make sense of our struggles. Some of us will face far greater struggles than others. And, it won't be fair. For reasons unknown, we all start out at different places in life. Each unique starting place presents each of us with our own unique struggles.

Yet, if we are enduring struggles (sadness, loneliness, worthlessness, uncertainty, exhaustion, even numbness), we might ask ourselves if it's something we did wrong, or some way in which we are deficient. Maybe this sounds silly as you're reading it. But what happens for you when your mind begins to focus on something you are struggling with? Due to human nature, and the way in which mental illness can influence our thoughts, you may look over at the person next to you and see them effortlessly moving along through life without this particular struggle that plagues you. Our first thought in that scenario is often, "why me?" or "I wish I wasn't..."

That instinct to highlight our own relative deficiency likely was not as common when we lived in small tribes and were more preoccupied with the ever-present threat of starvation. Maybe that's not true. Perhaps self-consciousness is an inherent part of being human that has been with us since the beginning of time. The argument here is that modern-day life amplifies this mirror that constantly follows us and helps us to feel bad. This automatic conclusion that we are doing something wrong, or worse, that we are inadequate in some way, only came along when life became easier. When life became easier overall, our expectations for ourselves increased by a lot. Because, well, life should be easy.

EXCEPTIONALISM AT ITS WORST

Yes, the 80s were a lot of fun. For most, but not all, prosperity reigned. There were very few immediate threats to our existence, so we turned our attention inward. Fear took advantage of this change in focus. Our collective mental health took a downward turn from there.

All that positivity and push towards self-improvement had a side effect. In pushing ourselves toward ever greater self- improvement, we got stressed out in the process. This drive to be exceptional, in one way or another, has remained. It still seems to be an unwritten need that permeates our society.

Instead of a making space inside ourselves to hold onto dreams and aspirations that also allows for patience and self-forgiveness, we require ourselves to be exceptional in one way or another. However, being better, or best, or even perfect, has been injected so deep into our psyches that we often can't even see it's there. There's little patience for the process of improving. This may be because 'improving' means you're not there yet. There's also little self-forgiveness for anything short of straight A's in school, and in life in general.

We have drifted a long way away from the simpler days of the mid-twentieth century. In 1953, the popular pediatrician D.W. Winnicott expressed the sentiment that we do not have to be perfect parents to raise our children well. She coined the term "the good enough mother." It's a profoundly important and impactful message. It would also make for a terrible blog title nowadays.

Exceptional seems to be the standard - one that we must not only aim for but have already achieved before making that first impression with anyone new. We walk through life as if others are about to ask us straight up, "Well, what makes you so special?" If we answer, "not much," clearly that would feel like a disappointing answer. Being regular is definitely not sexy or admirable. And, being sexy or admirable in some other way, often feels like the bare minimum.

Alternatively, there may be some degree of relief in being regular. It may just provide an escape hatch in the unfulfilling, impossible to survive, octagon of modern-day social competition.

This quest for exceptionalism also reflects our society's fantastical belief in our ability, perhaps even obligation, to master life's challenges and look good while doing it. In reality, the person behind all of our social media accounts is a real human being with very real problems and very real limitations. If that's not what comes across in the social media posts, we can ask, "why not exactly?"

Maybe since the vibe of most images on social media are exceptionalism oriented, we then feel obligated to go along. Maybe we have been influenced to do so. We are immersed in a culture driven by exceptionalism. The result? For most all of us, it's a perfection-seeking mentality that creates a lot of opportunity for us to become hypercritical of ourselves.

Self-criticism is real, and really common. Self-criticism is the final piece of the equation that makes the math work out. If others are so exceptional, and we are just regular, it makes sense if that's somehow our fault. Often, fear of inadequacy underlies our self-criticism. We can't turn off our brains' fear center. That actually wouldn't be a good idea. Job number one in life is survival. To stay safe, we need fear.

But perhaps we can avoid taking the bait that modern-day life tries to lure us in with. Signing up for exceptionalism culture can be a total set-up. Seeking exceptionalism may give us the feeling that we are in control. Moving towards a better body, a bigger bank account, a greater social media following feels good. It gives us the sense that we are moving forward, improving, gaining respect and admiration.

The opposite may actually be true. There is no calm when you are aching to be a different version of yourself. Any attachment to an idealized self...one that by default rejects our regular old self... is likely getting in the way of the key aspects of mental wellness... fulfilment, joy, a sense of peace. This discrepancy between our idealized self and our real self will use life's disappointments, failures, and conflicts to fuel criticism of ourselves and possibly others.

It's not all about social media, money, and six-pack abs either. Many of us seek a different kind of perfection. We take on a variety of jobs and responsibilities (parent, friend, caregiver, employee, among others) with the intention of getting it all done. Plus, there are bonus points for doing so with a "no big deal" attitude. It usually turns out to be a lot more work than we anticipated. We double down on our efforts, and later try to hide how hard it actually was.

We get it done, or at least most of it. Yet, in our minds, we fell short. Despite great effort and perseverance, we can't shake the feeling it was a failure. These expectations we place upon ourselves are often a little (or a lot) higher than what is reasonable.

THE BEAUTY OF HUMAN LIMITATIONS

Unfortunately, there are only so many hours in the day and only so much bandwidth in our brains. You may respond to this by saying to yourself, "not me... I can't get anything done... I can't focus... I can't keep up... I can't be what he/she wants me to be... I can't (fill in the blank)"

For many of us, this is a common internal conversation. This type of conversation we have with ourselves is often the root of anxiety, depression, or anger issues. It starts small but can grow exponentially. This is why mental illness conditions can be so impairing. If we are not mentally and emotionally well, then our mental health becomes our full-time job. Everything else, without regard for your desires or best intentions, comes second. This can be excruciatingly painful.

When that negative internal dialogue strikes, you likely will not be able to accomplish as much of your to- do list as you wanted. It would probably be a victory to get anything done at all, considering how you feel. That's because these conversations tend to play in our minds on repeat, 24/7.

Nonetheless, in your mind, you feel like you should be taking on a ton more responsibility and accomplishing way more. You may wonder if you're being a good enough friend now that you are laid low with depressed mood or heightened anxiety. You may look over at the kitchen sink and see a filthy pile of laziness and failure. The missed calls from work, friends, and even family, you could have answered, but didn't, may still produce pangs of guilt hours later.

Even when symptoms are less intense and we are more functional, our inability to get it all done can still be very painful. Here's why...our minds have this habit of setting a really high bar, which is due, in large part, to exceptionalism.

If we are not mentally well, it would make more sense to deal with that first, then worry about our productivity. Similarly, if you had a rock in your shoes it would make sense to stop and take it out, instead of ignoring the rock and learning to cope by walking on your toes and dosing ibuprofen every six hours. But the modern-day playbook in regard to our mental and emotional health tends to be just that: ignore the pain, double down on the effort, pretend it's all good on the outside, try to distract from the pleas to stop coming from within.

Due to many factors in modern-day life, and our own innate, fear- fueled drive to survive, we tend to set very high expectations for ourselves. These expectations are often too high, or at least unreasonable or misguided. The higher the expectations, the more effort we have to put forth. The more effort we have to put in, the greater the degree of burnout. The greater the burnout, the worse we perform. The worse we perform, the worse we feel about ourselves. But we don't stop. If we do, we've failed.

Why would we do this ourselves? Why are we breaking our backs to be exceptional when all that does is just inevitably lead us to be exceptionally miserable? It's possible that we are trying to be exceptional because deep down we believe it will solve a different problem.

Six-pack abs are awesome. But are they the solution to loneliness? Working hard and earning good money is great. But can it alone make our past hurts, disappointments, or failures simply vanish? Social media likes offer us that quick dopamine hit. But do they boost our sense of self-worth in a lasting way?

Stress management starts with a perspective change. Instead of wondering where we went wrong in failing to be that superhero, it may be more beneficial in the long run (and for everyone around us) to stop and take a minute to sit with the idea that we don't have to be all that to be connected and respected. We are human, which means we have faults. However, we're all still invited to the party despite our differences. Yes, even you.

We have limitations – it's okay to show them to others. It's actually what makes us unique and likeable. We cannot ask for and receive help if we hide our limitations. We all need help, sometimes. We all need connection and to be seen, always.

When things go south or we begin to struggle, we take on the task of fixing things all by ourselves, in secret, in our dark emotional hiding place, with the gentleness and compassion of a sledgehammer. Maybe after a perceived failure, in this darkness, we tell ourselves to "try harder," or that we need to "fix it," or worse, we go numb. That's the approach we take when we buy into exceptionalism.

To achieve better control over our stress, perhaps we have to start by making tough choices about which self-improvement endeavors and life responsibilities are a priority, and which are not.

This doesn't mean that we shouldn't try at all in life. We need stress. Stress builds resilience. In short spurts, it helps make us stronger. Stress is the means to build strength, improve, and learn. The key is striking a balance between nothing and everything. This balanced middle path allows us room to grow, but avoids the hypercritical drive towards exceptionalism. To accomplish this, we have to go by feel.

LEARN TO MANAGE YOUR MANAGER

We will always have stress. It's unavoidable. Not all stress, however, is worth the cost. Trying to be exceptional comes with a hefty price tag. It often fails to pay off as well.

There's a famous business adage, "you can't manage what you don't measure". This relates to our drive toward exceptionalism. Most exceptionalism goals these days are quantifiable. Nowadays, we tend to think about of quality of life in terms of the quantities we have in life - the amount of money, friends & followers...the ranking of our schools, companies, & cars... the speed at which we can get things done, either by us or for us. Quantity seems to be the new quality.

We are definitely managing our life through measuring. But, are we using the right measuring tape? For most of us, there's a set of numbers in our mind that nag us. Maybe it's the numbers in the bank account, maybe it's the number on the scale, maybe it's the number of friends...or social media followers...or past sexual partners...or people that directly report to you at work.

Safe to say that there's usually a number involved. If this is true for you, then what problem did you think getting to that number would solve?

Whatever that number is, consider how your life would be different if we lived in a world where getting to that number made no difference whatsoever. Imagine if we had a way of measuring the intangible blessings of life with numbers. Remember, as a kid, you would tell the people who cared for you, with arms stretched out wide, that you loved them "thiiiissssss muuucchhhh"? In numbers, how much was that exactly?

Relationships, experiences, and passions in life cannot be measured with any sort of number. It's easy to get hyper-focused on numbers. But numbers can't hug you back. Only people can hug you back. Maybe the one number we should focus on is the number of hugs, real and metaphorical, we give and get each day.

We obviously have to put in work to get those six-pack abs or that six-figure salary. But, we also have to put in work in our relationships to get the point where hugs are a common occurrence and feel good every time.

You are your own manager. As a manager, it's wise to measure. When it comes to mental health, measuring quantities of things, however, is nowhere near as helpful as measuring the value of experiences, the quality of our relationships, the depth of our own self-acceptance, and the degree to which we can know and appreciate our own uniqueness. Do this, and you will likely gain more clarity over which stressors provide no value and therefore should be avoided, or at least taken way less seriously. Think about what's happening and who's around when you have felt good.

In sum, exceptionalism takes away more than it gives back. Exceptionalism related stressors should be pushed aside. There are stressors, however that we should not avoid because they do provide value. For these kinds of stressors, the ones that are worth it, the well-known stress management techniques will come in handy.

THAT ITCH YOU CAN'T SCRATCH

Mindfulness and meditation are so hot right now, and for good reason. These techniques are potentially life changing. But they are tools, not magic potions. Mindfulness and meditation practices need to fit into a certain mindset in order to foster substantial positive change. If used as spot treatments in a crazed, super stressful, exceptionalism driven lifestyle, the results will definitely be lackluster.

We are mistaken if we think we can manage all of our stress by allowing it free rein throughout our daily mental landscape and then taking 10 minutes out of our day to close our eyes and meditate. Doubling the dose to 20 minutes of meditating won't work either.

The answer (periodic meditation sessions) doesn't match the problem (overdoing it while being hellbent on exceptionalism). Has eating whatever you want all day, then going for a 10- minute walk to try to burn off all those extra calories, ever worked for anyone trying to manage their weight?

Here's the problem... during meditation, you allow whatever thoughts to bubble up to your consciousness. Bringing down your defenses during meditation may actually allow in negative thoughts, memories, and mood states.[89] That makes sense if you are drowning in stress and pressure.

If you take time out to sit quietly with yourself, you may discover that you are truly afraid or disturbed by something in your life. Whatever bothers you was likely there the whole time. It's just that your busy mind never allowed it access to center stage. Meditation pulled back the curtain. If you are a busy person, meditation may just allow all your daily pressures, insecurities, guilt, and shame free access to your consciousness. What used to be stored underground suddenly bubbles up to the surface.

Generally, it's good to process our repressed emotions, so we can eventually let them go. But the unexpected arrival of difficult thoughts and feelings can be surprising or unsettling. Meditation can easily open up a can of worms, and there's no guarantee that it can clean it all up in the same 10-minute session.

TIME SPENT IS TIME EARNED

Traditional cultures have given us an array of stress reduction techniques and restorative practices. Various traditions that have found a place in popular culture today – meditation, yoga, long distance running, saunas, and even prayer. However, back when traditional culture invented and refined these stress management practices, people had more time on their hands.[90]

People were busy bailing hay, not spending hours shopping for better fitting underwear online. There were fewer in-your-face distractions. There were fewer choices to make - and none with seemingly unlimited options. Life afforded so much more solitude and time for reflection. Modern-day life had not arrived yet to provide a 24-hour news cycles, flashing neon lights, smart phone notifications, and easy access to an all-you-can-eat buffet of vices. Modern-day life gave us more to do and less time to do it.

Although people faced some serious and dangerous threats, their stress was likely not as amplified and diversified as it is today. It was likely that eating, sleeping, reproducing, and staying safe were the primary concerns back then. Currently, it is important to earn good grades or a good living, while also being a good parent/child/sibling/friend, and at the same time being fashionable, like-able, witty, smart, giving, profoundly wise, technologically savvy, up to date on the trends... and the list goes on. Life was likely boring enough to make meditation, yoga, long distance running, and prayer the highlight of your day rather than the footnote.

Part of the problem with our modern-day understanding of ancient traditions is that today these techniques are taught as skills that can be practiced in short, discrete sessions. Applying these practices into short periods of your modern-day life just may not be enough if the rest of your day is filled with deadlines, pressure, perceived (or real) criticism, lack of acknowledgement, self-judgment, and negative emotions that have no way out. You may have heard the expression, "that's like bringing a squirt gun to a house fire".

How can someone suddenly stop the madness in their mind and immediately find their way into a Zen state? To accomplish that would require practice – years of an hours-a-day practice.

THE UPSIDE OF BEING NEGATIVE

The personalities that promote meditation, mindfulness, yoga, and related practices frequently present as super chill and totally enlightened. So then we try it out. Meditation session number one is a bust. Bringing our mind's awareness into our bodies is like trying to jam a cat into its carrier. Our thoughts seem to fight tooth and nail to go back to our normal daily routine of scattered busyness. Cats are stubborn and so are our minds.

We sit and breathe, but despite our best effort, all that bubbles up for us is the things on our to do list and the other long list of things that are currently stressing us out. If something negative came up for us, or we just couldn't focus, that might give us the impression that we are doing it wrong.

As a beginner, this is likely more the norm than the exception. As human beings, we were gifted a really powerful brain that can, with relative ease and impressive might, feel bad. It's strange to think of sadness or fear as gifts, but without these important emotional experiences, we'd be walking through life without a clue. Fear is why no one walks up to lions and tigers to try and pat them on the head. Similarly, fear of loneliness is why no one is ever honest when asked by their friends how their outfit looks.

It's not our fault when we feel something intensely. It means that our brains are working as designed by evolution. Just being happy and positive all the time is like flying in a plane that never lands. That might sound like an amazing alternative to what's happening in your life, but all that positivity would get old quick. Indeed, our brains were designed to absorb and cling to the negative.[91]

If we were ignorant or unaware of the risks around us, we could not protect ourselves from the bad things that might happen to us. We need to be aware of the negative to find ways to navigate around it. If certain experiences or relationships didn't make us feel bad, we might never learn to avoid them.

The flip side of this protective mechanism is that if we're not carefully observant, we can easily drown in our fears. As stressful, threatening, or hurtful situations come up in life, we undoubtedly feel it. As modern life gains greater influence over us, these protective brain mechanisms are triggered far too often. Like over-reactive smoke detectors in your kitchen, our brains can easily get set off by modern-day life.

Negativity is there to keep us aware of possible dangers in the environment. It's one of our many tools in life. Predicting the negative is indicative of a fully functioning imagination. But this can go too far, too fast. Allowing yourself to be convinced that some negative outcome is most definitely, for sure going to happen is a failure of another part of your brain. That would be the decision-making center in your brain, called the frontal cortex (more on this later in the book).

Even research that stemmed from the father of stress management, Richard Lazarus, concludes that problem-focused coping leads to better physical and emotional outcomes for people, when compared to emotion-focused coping.[92] You can't work through your problems if you don't face them. You won't face your problems if the flood of emotions are too much at the time, or if you spend most of your time trying to block out the pain.

In other words, sometimes we need a healthy dose of denial to get through tough days. But at some point, we need to stop, go back and deal with our stuff. Like the quote attributed to Woody Guthrie, we have to "take it easy, but take it." Taking action helps us proceed without the invisible anchors of fear, regret, guilt, & shame.

LESS IS MORE

In modern-day life, we have less time to meet a greater number and complexity of expectations. If we fall short, we feel bad. We feel like we failed somehow. Many of us carry around this disappointment in ourselves for not being better. Rarely do we remind ourselves that we are imperfect human beings that are perfect just the way we are. We are supposed to have weaknesses to complement our strengths. If we didn't have any flaws, we'd be creepy robot zombies.

When it comes to stress management, the lesson seems to be that less truly is more. The less we bombard ourselves with persistent electronic stimuli, the less we take on unnecessary tasks, the less we exhaust ourselves with excessively long to-do lists, the more we will feel alive and well.

With strong guard walls built up against the dangerous tentacles of modern-day life, we can spend more time being present and focusing on the good in ourselves and in our lives. We should establish those boundaries with exceptionalism first, then try to meditate.

Meditation doesn't just automatically calm us down. In some instances, it unearths uncomfortable feelings that we have to push down to be able to get on in day to day life. So instead of producing an immediate sense of serenity and oneness with the world, it can actually do the opposite. Therefore, meditation is not a passive sport.

Meditation typically doesn't go according to plan. Without fail, as we meditate, our minds wander. We are supposed to be focused on our body and our breathing, but inevitably we drift. As your mind wanders, where will it go? Where it goes is actually one of the best gifts that meditation has to offer.

If we feel, think, or remember something bad when we meditate... that's not a sign that we are doing it wrong. Meditation is the most important mirror in our lives. It will show us who we are, what's been on our mind and in our heart, what we need to let go, and where we feel we want to go in life. If we listen and follow where our thoughts drift, it will tell us what we need to hear. It doesn't take us somewhere else, somewhere better. It doesn't transform us into something more.

Drugs, binge watching TV, online shopping, daydreaming, and all other kinds of vices change the channel in our minds, so we never have to listen to what's really going on inside. This is why it's so important to cleanse ourselves of the toxic load dumped upon us from exceptionalism. It's better to rid ourselves of the unnecessary suffering of modern-day life before we try to manage our stress. Or, at least, we need to avoid the expectation that yoga, meditation, or any other technique can help us achieve our idealized self (perfection).

Once we get to this point of 'less is more', meditation can offer us a unique opportunity to forgive and accept ourselves as we are. On a physical level, meditation helps to reset our nervous system. A balanced nervous system helps to regulate our gastrointestinal system, immune system, and hormonal system.[93] On a more mental or spiritual level, meditation will unveil your humanness and vulnerability. That can help you be more balanced emotionally.

Recommendation:

HOW TO MEDITATE:

Meditation was born out of Buddhist tradition. Ayurvedic medicine provides us with breathing techniques and yoga. From these ancient cultures we are blessed with plenty of great methods out there. Meditation, yoga, tai chi, qi gong, exercise, prayer... it's not likely that one is clearly better than the next. Whatever you prefer will probably work best, as you're more likely to stick with it.

Yet, meditation is not always a positive experience. You'll know that it's working when it alerts you to the stress in your life. When you can more clearly see how certain stress is harming you rather than enhancing you, that's when change can happen.

If you sit down, begin meditating, and then find that your mind wanders, realize that's what's supposed to happen. Gently pull your thinking and awareness to whatever part of your body you wish - typically your lungs or nose. When weird stuff, uncomfortable thoughts, painful memories, or perceived inadequacies come up, just bookmark them for later. Later, ask yourself a few more questions about those thoughts and feelings.

This is how change happens. This is the transformative power of meditation. It's not the fantastical belief that meditating regularly will make you feel and become totally awesome. Meditation is an opportunity to seek & destroy the unnecessary layers of self-doubt and obligation to exceptionalism that hide in plain sight in our lives.

The responsibility that comes with a meditation practice is identifying, then banishing, the toxic attachments we hold to our idealized self, which are so rampant in modern-day life.

If you're feeling terrible and overwhelmed, perhaps distracting yourself with a walk around the block, a funny movie, or a new pair of shoes may be the best first step. If you're in a stable place, but don't necessarily have time to fall apart during the middle of the day, consider exercise, yoga, walking, and socializing. If you have the time and support structure to deal with difficult emotions, then consider meditation as a means to get closer to your emotions, not further from them.

Instead of setting a goal to do 10-20 straight minutes to daily meditation, try to fit mindfulness and other stress reduction techniques in the in-between moments. Stuck in traffic? Interrupt your focus on the insanely slow drivers ahead and remind yourself to breathe deeply, leading with your belly. Late night dishes piling up in the sink? Tackle it with mindful attention and presence. Focus on the water flowing over your hands, the suds bubbling over, and the sheen of the pots and pans as you place them on the rack... and don't forget to breathe. Waiting forever in line for your latte? Take a moment to go inward and see if you can feel your lungs moving or your heart beating in your chest.

A stress reducing, mindfulness reset actually only takes just a couple seconds. Deep breathing is pretty intuitive. Inhale, hold, then exhale, hold, and repeat. But there's a piece to it that most of us miss. Most of us don't realize it, but in modern-day life, we are so bombarded by environmental stressors and perceived threats, that we remain tense and breathe very shallow.

Notice if you breathe in & out with just your chest. Does your belly move at all? If you catch yourself breathing shallow... all chest, no belly... that may be a reflection of how tense you are throughout your body and brain. It's as if we are in a constant state of flinching.

HOW TO BREATHE:
Before you even attempt meditation, it's important - and immediately helpful – to learn how to breathe. Breathing may sound too simple of a thing to make a difference. But it's not. Breathing in

slowly, deeply, and with a relaxed body can change the activity in emotional centers of the brain - for the better.

Filling your belly with air is pretty intuitive. Loosen the belt a notch if you need to, then let you belly expand outward as well as sideways.

Next, focus on exhaling. A deep inhalation will fill up your chest. It creates a tension. That tension will help usher out the inhaled air without much effort. But, here's the key: as the air leaves your torso, focus on your shoulders. Let them drop down. As your shoulders sink, feel the tingle all the way up your spine and neck. For this one moment, let down your perma-guard. Your body and your brain will thank you.

HOW TO PRIORITIZE:

Once we rid ourselves of drives towards fruitless exceptionalism, where should we focus all this extra energy and attention?

First, get accustomed to the idea that you are unique, and that uniqueness makes you totally awesome. Seriously, no one else sees the world from your angle. That has value. Because of that unique perspective on life, no one else can offer what you can.

Second, focus on relationships! Without others, we are useless bags of bones and chemicals. Living life surrounded by people (and pets) that know us and like us (despite getting to know us) the only context in which we can be mentally and emotionally well.[94] These relationships can be leveraged to overcome sadness, disappointment, grief, loss, worries, fear, and any sort of dysfunction or perceived failure.

Nurture your friendships. Find an activity that you enjoy. Learn to sit with yourself in quiet. Have tough conversations with yourself before those issues get in the way of your relationships with others. Listen to music, preferably with others. Try to be with people and experiences that make you smile and laugh. Again, pets count too.

Learn to say "no" when needed. Learn to say "no" especially when it comes to the lure of modern-day life. Learn to say "no" to goals born from a toxic idealized-self. Learn to say "yes" to opportunities for fun, for connection and conversation, for challenge and growth. The important thing is to try to incorporate stress management with a sense of what you're ready for and what you're not.

LET'S SUMMARIZE...
Determine for yourself what stress in your life is worthwhile. Try to discard the rest.

Exceptionalism seems to be almost unavoidable in our modern-day life. It pushes us to take on roles and responsibilities that are not really that beneficial, and definitely not a requirement for others to like or respect us. In fact, the opposite is often true.

Think of those excess roles, responsibilities, and reputations as sugar. None is optimal. Some is tasty and relatively harmless. A lot pleases some part of our mind but is toxic in the long run.

Limit your exposure to useless stress by starting to accept your inherent self- worth and avoid trying to make yourself into something exceptional.

Practice self-forgiveness for all that you are not. Be fairer in your expectations of yourself.

Have fun. Be a closer and better friend. Ask for others to come hang out so they can do the same. Give more hugs, even to yourself. Open up and talk about your problems with those close to you.

Eat good food! (see recipes below)

Community:

We can't do it alone. We human beings need interaction with other human beings. Connection is an essential nutrient. We need to be able to rely upon each other. This interdependency stems from our evolutionary roots as a species. We flourished in tribes,[95] but currently in modern-day society, we find ourselves more and more alone.

Unfortunately, as described above, many stress management practices assume that you are alone. Do an image search for anything related to meditation online, and you'll find hundreds of pics of a person with a folded leg silhouette, palms up to the sky, finger meeting the thumb, against a serene sunset backdrop. Looks beautiful, but also lonely, boring, and not really relative to everyday life. Typically, starting out in mindfulness involves a lot of distractions, discomfort, and doubts – the opposite of what that image is trying to convey.

Breathing exercises, meditation, or any mindfulness technique is best performed in private. That's problematic. When you're in the mix, work and life responsibilities are coming at you from right and left, people in your life are demanding your attention right then and there, it's unreasonable to expect yourself to be able to abruptly shut off and go straight to your happy place with ease and grace.

Can you imagine yourself in a meeting with your boss at work, maybe your quarterly performance review, and it's not going well? You can tell your boss is displeased and about to eat you for lunch. But, you stop, close your eyes, go inward, and imagine yourself nailing a perfect tree pose on a warm secluded beach. Breathe in, hold, exhale, hold. Namaste. You're now practicing, with full intention, your uber powerful stress reduction technique. Repetitively inhaling until your belly protrudes as far out as it can go, then with a deep "hawwwuuuhhhhhh," all while your boss is staring at you, waiting for you to finish up. Doesn't sound that practical, does it? Perhaps this is why your boss wants to talk to you about your performance at work.

To avoid any confusion, there is definitive value to these ancient practices.[96] They are tools that have their time and place. That time and place is when you have the time and space. Mindfulness practices should be part of your everyday life. Attending to your breathing pulls you out of your monkey mind and back into your body where you belong. Yoga increases physical and mental strength.

Running is good for your heart and mind. Carving out time will make a big difference in your life. But these practices have limitations.

Since there's only a select set of times and places you can engage in these practices, what else could help during these times when the whole day is such chaos? What could help distract you from your problems long enough to get in a good laugh and the confidence to continue to submit C+ work at your job? Your friends!

Meditation can calm down your nervous system and give you the poise in the moment you need it the most. But, in truth, meditation can't always build you back up the way that friends and family can. Meditation and other mindfulness techniques have nothing on good old venting sessions with your BFF.

We likely have all made it through some difficult and challenging times with the help of our friends. And, these are the friends who don't exactly practice active listening. Rather than summarizing what we just said and reflecting back our emotions – as the textbooks say we should – our most ride or die friends allow us to momentarily blame others for our problems. What a gift!

In these moments of need, they fail to help us take real responsibility for our mistakes. They are biased, and their lack of solid evidence for this support gives us the confidence to go back out in the world and try another day. We might be in the wrong, but they'll still be behind us.

It's loyalty over logic when it comes to close friends, sibling, mothers, fathers, hair stylists/barbers. We all need a healthy dose of this. At a certain point, a good friend will let your know when you're really off track. But, typically that's about year 10 into a relationship.

There are two important points to remember here. First, solitude is a good thing, in measured doses. It is critically important for us to be able to be alone with ourselves. Spiritual journeys or solo quests have traditionally been a part of the human experience. There is something transformative and invaluable about walking the path in the dark woods by yourself and coming out the other side a changed person.

Second, although solitude has its place, community and support from others is massively important to our mental and emotional wellbeing. When you come down the mountain from your spiritual quest with a beard down to your chest, it's much more meaningful if you can regale your friends with stories of your journey. Likewise, catching up on what you missed in their lives while you were gone is also part of the healing nature of relationships. We just need connection in our lives to feel and be well. Community and support from others close to us is very protective against mental illness.[97-98]

The problem with modern life is the absence of opportunities to connect in real ways with others. Real connection sometimes means that kind of listening, empathy, and support that has blatant disregard for the facts. It includes eye contact, nodding, unhappy pouty faces, and near excessive use of the words "literally... seriously... totally... dude... girl... & bro."

What can easily happen instead in modern-day life, is that we are all too often mindlessly hanging out with each other. Instead of listening with attention, our minds wander or our eyes search for our phone and other screens. When others are expressing pain and frustration, it's not always easy to hold that space.

Those in-between moments have become hard for us, in part because of the bounty of distractions that invade our everyday lives. When conversations hit a lull, we often fall back into our monkey mind. Constantly returning to our ever-expanding to-do list in our mind is a hard habit to break.

It feels like an undying thirst for any kind of input into our thinking brain. Things that excite, entertain, reward, or even irritate you all have the power to capture your attention. Their grip is tight. These distractions distance us from the people in our lives. Even when we do listen, we sometimes fall into the trap of trying to fix everything so we (and everyone else around us) don't have to go through the pain of feeling anything negative.

Similarly, when we begin to feel depressed, or anxious, or mentally foggy, our first instinct can be to suppress, ignore, and just try to push on through. In the absence of others in our lives – listening to us, talking to us, supporting us, seeing our pain – we recede inward. We are then always walking the path alone, which is a risky way to go. It sets us up for depressed moods, anxious thoughts, and a distracted mind.

In modern-day life, we can be surrounded by people, and totally alone at the same time. Loneliness is a kind of anemia. We need connection in our daily life, just like we need iron and other vitamins, to have energy and feel well.

Recommendation:

As mentioned in the section on stress management, making an effort to nurture your relationships with friends, with family if you can, or even with pets is an important step to improving our mental and emotional wellbeing.

If you feel like this doesn't relate to you, like you just don't have any friends so this whole section is a pass, please hold on a second. The time for making new connections and finding new ways to be social is always. The past never dictates the future. We can always start over. There are millions and millions of people out there, so many millions of people. You can't possibly be alone with what you're experiencing. If you're human, then you experience things that humans experience, and that means there are others out there that can relate. Those people tend to make the best new friends. If you try, you may just find them.

Where to begin? We can start by thinking about the difference between doing and being. Doing leads to results. Being doesn't. But being is not about results. There's no need to do anything when we are being who we already are. Think about your plans for the week. Do you schedule in time for meandering walks, tinkering with stuff at home, playing an instrument or games? Or do you tend to think about planning as only including productive activities that require as little in-depth communication with others as possible, so as to ensure maximal productivity?

What's an alternative? Less doing equals more being. Avoiding the urge to do means that you are just left to be yourself without any need to be something more. Less planning things we want to accomplish, more planning to just hang out. Start by adding time with others to the to-do list for the week. The danger is that the more we are doing, the less we are being. Then who we are as an individual may become somewhat foreign to us. If we put more time into being and going with the flow, we may experience more happiness. If you're happier, maybe it will make you more productive overall.

Also, consider being more of an open book. It's definitely scary to think about being more honest about your wants or your warts. But doing so often draws people in. Think about the alternative. What commonly pushes others away is the outward appearance of perfection. If you are perfect and exceptional, there's nothing for others to grab onto in the relationship. Where's the drama? Where's the intrigue? Where's the relatability? What would there be to talk about? Connection with others is vitally important. It starts with self-acceptance. Try it out!

Sleep:

If you had a PC in the 1990s, you were probably prompted by Microsoft Windows to perform the occasional disk defragmentation. It's still unclear to me what that was all about, but the program would pop up and display a random series of colored blocks. By the time it was finished, all the blocks were neatly grouped by color. I suppose the point was to consolidate and organize all your data in a way that improved efficient access to that data later on.

Can't argue with that logic. When you're about to walk out your front door, it's always easier to grab your keys if you put them in the same spot every time you come home. It's about efficient access and retrieval. Something very similar occurs in our brains when we sleep.

As we progress through the various stages of sleep, from light sleep, to deep sleep, to dreaming, our brains consolidate and organize information gathered earlier that day.[99-100] Sleep helps us store memories and encode new information.[101]

In addition, brain activity during sleep builds wisdom as it makes meaningful connections between all those pieces of information we took in during the day.[100] On the way to making all those meaningful connections in the dream state, things get weird. But it's a good weird. By the time we wake up, your brain hashed out all the craziness and is in a much better position to respond to life.

All that digesting of life's experiences is important for emotional regulation.[102] Being human, we experience a lot of emotions in a day. Some good, some (maybe a lot) bad. Intense emotions stem from difficult or ugly situations. Situations tend to stick around for a while, emotions well up inside, but can also pass on by. It's often how we look at a situation that either keeps an emotion front and center, or lets it fade away.

Emotional regulation is the ability to look at a situation from different angles, like turning a jagged stone over in your hand. From one angle, what you see makes you infuriated. Turn it over, and you can see another side that maybe makes you feel sad or hurt. Turn it over once more, and you can now see a totally different angle that helps you feel empathy and understanding. Our brain practices this sort of emotional regulation during sleep. Sleep helps us process our experiences and put them in the right place. This is likely where the saying, "just sleep on it," comes from.

Good, quality sleep brings wisdom and fresh energy. We need that wisdom and energy for tackling our many unavoidable problems. When problems come at us, we can run, duck, and hide. Or we can take them on. If we take them on, we will feel stuff... generally intense, dark, uncomfortable, icky stuff. Courtesy of a good night's sleep, however, we are more emotionally regulated and take life in smaller bits. Emotional regulation helps us to put the pieces of the puzzle together in a rational and productive way.

The alternative to emotional regulation is raw emotions that surge up from below and catch us off guard. These upwellings of emotion frequently make us irrational. Then we overreact. Ironically, this surge of emotion starts with suppression. The opposite of turning over the stones to make more sense of the situation, is suppression.

This is when we initially stuff our feelings and never make an effort to try and go back to them in order to better understand them. The cycle of suppression starts with pretending the problem doesn't exist. But it does exist, and at some point stuffing it just doesn't work any longer. Then we generally have a freak out. After freaking for a while, we end up exhausted. The emotion subsides, but without a resolution, we walk around with a pit in our stomach because we know it's not over. Next thing we know, something triggers those feeling again and the freak out cycle continues.

Without effectively processing what is going on for us, we may become victims of overwhelming negative emotions later on. We know this, but we also operate at times as if we don't know it's true. We can get triggered and not have any idea what's wrong or why we're so upset.

If you never defragment your disk in your sleep, or in therapy, or in self-reflection, you're bound to jam up your brain. That's not only frustrating and confusing, it prevents our forward progress in life.

Beyond this emotional regulation thing, sleep helps regenerate brain structures and improve function,[103-105] as well as removing wastes from the brain.[106-107] There really is no optimal brain function without an adequate amount of undisturbed sleep. Good, quality sleep keeps your brain healthy and functioning optimally. Sleep is the ultimate reset button. Check it out!

Recommendation:

The classic advice is to aim for 8 hours. But, more recent research points to 7 hours as the new minimum, which is kind of helpful in our busy modern-day lives.[108] If you struggle to fall asleep, try to limit or avoid lights from electronic devices.[109] Try to decrease the temperature in your bedroom as well. The optimal range is between 63 and 65 degrees Fahrenheit.[110] It does sound cold, but dropping the temperature cues the body to initiate the sleep sequence that is restorative for our body and brain.

Preparation for sleep requires some attention as well. If you can go full speed all day long and then climb into bed and instantaneously fall asleep as soon as you head hits the pillow, that could be a sign that you're overdoing it. Your body may be near the point of exhaustion.

Attend to your sleep needs by preparing an hour or two before. Set a cutoff time when you stop responding to emails, turn off the television, and avoid petty arguments with loved ones. Maybe even pick up a book (not this one, a boring one). Again, remember that modern life is the villain here. It's pulling you towards less sleep, more stress, greater inner tension, worse nutrition, and more conflict. In modern-day life, our brain is outnumbered.

We have so many options for distractions in our homes. Less is more. Lean into sleepy time by slowing down your activity and your brain will follow.

Meaning and Purpose:

ALL TIME HIGH
Hopefully this text will encourage you to take the leap of faith and start eating better, moving more, protecting your sleep, and reaching out to others. My hope is that these efforts will change your life. I want you to feel more energized, think more clearly, and perform better in life.

Yet, you might be asking yourself, what's the point? What's it all for? TMWD nutrition and lifestyle guidance may just help you feel and function better or relieve mood and anxiety issues. Eating all this brain food no doubt helps me perpetually achieve high scores in whatever addictive smart phone game I'm sucked into at the moment. But, we can aim higher.

Discovering a higher purpose may actually help to prevent backsliding. Diet always starts Monday, am I right? With a strong purpose, something greater than yourself, you may be more likely to keep discipline and forward motion going by Tuesday. Hopefully, when you're fighting for something bigger, you'll be better able to keep up these good habits forever!

The highest aim of TMWD is to help you sever the mental and emotional anchors that are pulling you down. What do you think is preventing you from reaching your highest potential? Are there physical ailments? Is it brain fogginess? Are painful emotional states weighing you down? Is it self-doubt based on a series of past failures (or at least perceived failures)?

The premise of this book is that following the wisdom plucked from traditional cultures and now backed by science will help you live a better life. In large part, it's about what we need to eat to best fuel our brain – the organ most responsible for how we feel and perform.

Although, if you haven't noticed already, this book about nutrition has a lot of touchy-feely sentiments scattered throughout. Coming from the field of psychiatry, perhaps that was unavoidable for me. However, when we think about it, our experiences, thoughts, reflections, feelings, and interactions with others are all inputs into the system, just like all of our food choices. We can't just have a great diet but not pay attention to the other inputs, and then expect to remain mentally well. Similarly, we need that extra something in our life that helps us want to get out of bed in the morning. That extra something is meaning and purpose.

All of the guidance in TMWD is here to lift you up so that you can, in turn, do more for yourself and others. Why else would we go through the trouble of eating organ meat, staring into the sun first thing in the morning and passing on late night television show binges? We do it for love. Love for ourselves and the people in our lives that benefit from that love and attention.

If you feel disconnected from family, feel like you have no friends, or can't related to the concept of a 'support system', hope is not lost. Everyone has something to offer. We just need to find out what your unique ways of seeing the world are. That one-of-a-kind perspective is your undeniable gift to the rest of us. We will be better because of it, we just have to get to know you first.

Here's a warning, however. Following TMWD and finding your purpose will not make life easier. We put in the work and we get better. Then a strange thing happens. Once we become better at a certain skill, gain comfort with managing our tasks, or feel more confident in handling all of our responsibilities, life just throws us even greater challenges. Our only option then is to continue to try and overcome.

The good news is that this never-ending mountain climb is beneficial for our mental health. Living to our fullest potential is a journey, not a destination. Although we may never get "there," the act of striving is an essential feature of being human.[111-112]

But how can we strive, if we are so weighed down with mental illness? The goal of TMWD is to no longer feel yourself dragging through the days, no longer feel trapped in cycles of negativity in your mind, no longer feel like you have to hide the fact that a dense brain fog has disabled your brain and sapped your joy. We can start with food and our lifestyle habits. We then have to keep going to find out what makes us tick.

DON'T HIDE & GO SEEK

Human beings were designed a certain way. We're always seeking. We needed to be oriented towards reward seeking and risk taking to survive and thrive. It was, and in some ways still is, a requirement for survival. Mating, hunting, fighting or fleeing, befriending, cooperating, and mating again were the principles humans lived by for centuries. Civilization changed the landscape, and physical challenges were replaced with more complex and insidious psychological ones.

Nowadays, we don't need to hunt, or even really need to get out of our cars to get food. Feeling accepted as a member of a group seems more challenging nowadays compared to our tight knit tribal ancestors who needed each other for basic survival. I'm referring to our modern-day plagues of implicit biases, office politics, the geographic spreading out of families, and general divisiveness that we are all harmed by in one way or another.

Life has surely changed, but our brain configuration has not. The reward pathways that drove us towards survival, reproduction, and group cohesion are still there. It's just that these reward pathways seem to be occupied with different aims. In this context of a fast and furious, relatively safe (clearly not safe for everyone), modern-day life, we have developed the bad habit of seeking instant gratification. Not all instant gratification is bad, but it's about how we can easily begin to lean on instant gratifications too much.

Alternatively, you may actually be the kind of person that feels allergic to instant gratification. You may be very fearful of it or worried that if you ever let up off the throttle, you'll fall into immediate destitution for the remainder of your life. Sounds dramatic, but this fear is very real for many people, especially younger people nowadays. If you constantly focus on putting resources into your future and never stop to have fun, then obviously you are geared more towards delayed gratification.

Neither of these extremes serve us well. We are human beings, designed to seek out things that we think are good for us. Our brains are fine tuned to seek rewards. The problem is that our choices can be easily misguided in modern-day life. On the delayed gratification side, those rewards could be accomplishments, status, or financial security. On the instant gratification end, it could be multiple sexual partners, hyperpalatable food, drugs, expensive things, or any other hedonistic pleasure that you would lie to your primary care physician about.

Moderation and balance are key. It's okay to dabble in both instant and delayed gratification. Sticking solely or rigidly to just one or the other is a clear pitfall. Moving towards something in life that has a higher and longer lasting meaning is important. Working towards something bigger than yourself in life can help us avoid the pitfalls of both instant and delayed gratification. Meaning and purpose are more like medium gratification. Striving towards something bigger can be grueling and the payoff is often delayed somewhat. But it's also kinda fun and thrilling.

The seeking involved in dedicating ourselves to some purpose or goal higher or greater than ourselves is as good for us as it is for the benefactors of our good deeds. For us, it can help to sever the anchors of depressed or anxious thoughts, negative self-assessments, and feelings of emptiness. Further, it satisfies our deep-rooted need to seek rewarding experiences. And this seeking is neither selfish and impulsive, nor prudish and deathly boring. Meaning and purpose breathes life into your daily existence. This too is an essential daily nutrient.

Recommendation:

Wherever you are along the spectrum of depression, anxiety, or other mental distress, think about things you can do to discover meaning and purpose in your life.

If at this moment, your condition is more severe, then it may be a while before you can engage in meaning and purpose. In this case, you will need to address yourself first, and that's okay. Just don't give up, because the world still has big plans for you.

If you do feel like you have the energy and presence of mind, don't hesitate. Start to think about what moves you. All that attention into something greater than yourself may help you feel better right off the bat. Listen to your thoughts and reactions to things to find what drives you.

4 Step Guide to Finding Greater Purpose:

1. Start with the negative. Think about what makes you uncomfortable or upset. Is it starving children? Is it homeless animals? Do you wish there was better help out there for people dealing with the same problems afflicting you or your family members?

2. Think about how you could help yourself feel more comfortable with that issue. What can you do to try and change things? If you donated to charities that fed starving children, that might be a start. If you volunteered time taking care of shelter animals, you might find you're onto something. If you went back to school to learn more about how to help others like yourself or your family members, that might lead to a big change in how you feel about life and how you feel about yourself.

3. Whichever issue strikes a chord for you, try to find a challenge related to that issue. Make sure that it's not something easy. It's best if your purpose is a challenge that is impossible to master, something that may never be fully finished or accomplished. Think of the obsession some teens have for skateboarding, or the allure of golf for old guys. There's no perfect score in either of these endeavors. With a life's purpose, you will never be finished mastering your skill. There will always be more that can be done. Your work can never be finished. Although it sounds counterintuitive, this is a key element of one's meaning and purpose in life. As mentioned above, there is a certain kind of safety that comes with the never-ending nature of life's

challenges. It's not going anywhere, and neither are you. For many that can feel safe and fulfilling.

4. Finally, the meaning and purpose you choose will best serve you if it forces you to go against the grain. Doing something that someone else (or everyone else) is doing, won't give you that same feeling. It needs to feel lonely at times. It should also scare you a bit. You will persist, however. No one without your passion would want the job. That makes it yours. Since no one else dares try, it's only up to you to get it done. This solo quest can help inform your reason for existence, which also may help us feel safer and more at peace.

~ 5 ~

EVOLVING SCIENCE

Proof is in the randomized-controlled trial pudding

NUTRIENT DENSITY

Again, nutrient density is about maximizing our intake of nutrients needed for optimal brain and body function. There's obviously a limit to how many calories we can stomach in a day. Within that number of calories, it's a good idea to take in as many vitamins, minerals, amino acids, healthy fats, and other key nutrients as possible.

For example, French toast is a tasty treat, and it provides a ton of calories. But in terms of the nutrients needed for optimal brain function, that syrupy goodness pales in comparison to a square breakfast of eggs, meat, and potatoes with a side of spicy kimchi.

Many of the ancient foods described above may seem exotic and a little too far out there. However, one of the great things about nutrient density is that we don't need to consume a pound of beef liver, a dozen oysters, or a whole jar of sauerkraut every day to feel well. Just sprinkling these foods in among more commonly consumed whole foods, like fruits, vegetables, animal meats, and healthy fats can help round everything out.

If you can't tolerate the taste of some organs, shellfish, certain herbs and spices, fermented foods, or connective tissue foods, that's okay. TMWD provides options for supplement hacks to get your brain what it craves without the pangs of nausea.

KEY NUTRIENTS = OPTIMAL BRAIN FUNCTION

So far, we have established that traditional culture got a lot right. They either had an intuitive sense about what the human body and brain needed or just learned what to do through generations of trial and error. Eventually they figured out what worked best for diet and lifestyle. Things were good, minus the warfare, freezing winters, and occasional famine. Our ancestors lived in harmony with the seasons and the planet. We have lost touch with that harmony in modern-day life.

Living in harmony with the planet maximized our ancestors' brain power over time. They were able to use their newfound mental power to invent modern life. With an eye for speed, convenience, and ease of survival, people began to invent things and try to find ways to make hard parts of life easier. A couple of hundred years ago, after all that hard work and trying to make hard work less hard, the world changed dramatically over a relatively short period of time.

Food was easier to obtain, store, and consume. Work became less physical and more stationary. Communication and travel increased exponentially. Food started coming in boxes and cans instead of plucked from trees or picked from the ground. The hard work paid off and things were easier. But has it made life all around better?

Now, here we are in the middle of what seems like an epidemic of mental illness across all the developed nations of the world.[113] 1 in 5 people will experience mental illness this year. 20% of Americans meet the criteria for some sort of mental illness. And, only 50% of those American are currently receiving help.[114]

WHAT THE BRAIN NEEDS

Like most complex systems performing complex tasks, the brain needs more than just energy. So, in addition to fuel, our brains also require maintenance, protection, healthy structures, open lines of communication, and the resources to respond to life.

Meeting these five core needs of the brain depend on adequate nutrition and effective management of environmental stressors. Attend to each of these core needs well and you will foster an optimally healthy brain. Satisfying these basic needs will help us better respond to challenges in our lives. The remaining task is to decide how best to make meaning out of our experiences. Neither robots, nor zombies can do that. It's a human thing.

Life comes at us fast. We need a healthy and optimally functioning brain to deal with all of it. If you feel that you're struggling to cope, consider the following ways in which the brain is originally designed to function. These functions help us to cope with the daily onslaught of a changing environment that is rife with all kinds of threats and stressors.

Below is a quick preview of the budding science behind what keeps the gears moving in our brains. No surprise, a lot of that comes down to adequate nutrition and stimulation in life.

RESPOND:

The water's warm, jump on in. Life is happening all around us. When the symptoms of mental illness strike, we can feel disconnected, distracted, empty, nerve-wracked, or just 'blah.' These symptoms get in our way. If we aren't in the right state of mind to immerse ourselves in the experiences of life, we miss out.

We need to feel connected. We need to be able to feel life happening. But sometimes, we might need our emotional responses to be muted a little bit. We need volume dial control of our emotions. Feeling too much can be just as hard to deal with as not feeling enough. Which brain chemicals are responsible for managing our responding?

Neurotransmitters! They are the critical piece that needs to be in place in a healthy and optimally functioning brain in order for us to think, feel, reflect, interpret, remember, and respond with action. There are times and situations when we need our neurotransmitters to be there to help us feel connected to life. There are other times and situations when less is more, and we want the internal response to be more measured or even muted. It's not good when we get bogged down with intense feelings.

The systems that create (and later destroy) these neurotransmitters, so we can have the right amount at the right time, rely on two main things: key nutrients and the right kind of environmental stimulation.

BUILD:

Thinking takes time. At my house, figuring out what to eat for dinner takes a very long time. But less complex problem-solving typically takes just nanoseconds. Generally, we do best when our thinking and ability to process experiences occurs quickly and efficiently.

Neurons are the brain cells that do the communicating which allows us to have thoughts, feelings, and reactions to the world. By themselves, however, neurons send and receive messages relatively slowly. Myelin is the fatty substance that coats most neurons. This fatty coating that covers the entire length of most neurons is termed the myelin sheath. Its presence on neurons can mean the difference between a signal being carried 100 meters per second (with myelin sheath) and 1 meter per second (without myelin sheath).

Similarly, the outer membranes of neurons are vitally important to the quality and fidelity of messages sent and received inside the brain. We need healthy structures to keep the traffic in our brains' vast metropolises of chemical and electrical activity flowing swiftly, efficiently, and harmoniously.

As you may have guessed, there is an assortment of nutrients that support the growth and repair of these important structures. Getting them in your diet is crucial and takes some forethought.

FUEL:

We need energy. Without energy, we'd be a puddle of chemicals on the floor. That's because energy actually helps maintain our physical structure. Just as it takes energy for your body to stand upright and move around, your cells use energy to keep their borders intact and exchange the substances needed to keep their motors running. Mitochondria inside our neurons help provide the energy needed for them to grow, pass along messages, and branch out to make new connections.

Fuel is vital. If you don't have enough, you'll know it. Not only will you feel fatigued, but your mental sharpness will collapse into mental dullness. You'll be emotionally overwhelmed, your digestion and organ function may suffer, and you might even start gaining weight.

Again, the right nutrition is essential. Certain foods, much more than others, offer higher concentrations of the kinds of nutrients that promote energy creation. (Hint: it's not doughnuts.)

PROTECT:

Life is precious and so are our brains! The world is filled with infectious bugs and other serious toxins that have the potential to take us down. These invaders, once they breach the brain's initial defenses, can really jam up our mental functioning. Lucky for us, nature has provided us with an elaborate immune system nestled in and around the neurons. It clears up toxins, neutralizes infections, and sweeps away dead cells. It keeps our brain protected and safe.

Unfortunately, as with most things in life, too much of a good thing is a bad thing. Our brain wants the immune system to attack, but too much attacking can hamper brain function and even destroy healthy brain cells. Glial cells are the primary sentinels in the brain. They sense infections, toxins, and other problems that arise in the brain. Once alerted to a problem or intrusion, they spring into action.

This immune response uses fire to fight fire. If everything goes according to plan, the threat will be neutralized and soon your brain will return to its normal functioning. If overdone, however, our neurons can be harmed in the firefight. Balance is key. Certain nutrients and several lifestyle habits help keep the balance by providing an anti-inflammatory counterbalance that prevents our neurons from being overstimulated. Note that many modern-day foods contribute to furthering inflammation and should be avoided as much as possible.

BALANCE:
Once the brain has what it needs, it's time to fine tune the signals. Our brains truly are supercomputers. They can crunch a massive amount of data and organize it in a meaningful and useful way in short order. But sometimes there's interference in the signal. Excess activity leads to static that can drown out the important signals.

Think about your television. How many channels does your cable box provide? A thousand? But how many channels does your cable box let through to your television at a time? Just one. Our brains need to operate in a similar manner. There's a lot going on all around us, but we need to filter out the noise to be able to pick out the signal we want. Accomplishing that will help us find focus and peace.

The brain has a network of checks and balances to keep the activity humming along without interruption. As with every core function, these processes demand adequate nutrition to function optimally.

In sum, these core functions suffer from inadequate nutrition, lack of stimulation, or too much stress on their respective systems.

When these systems suffer, we suffer the consequences – mental and emotional dysfunction.

~ 6 ~

RESPOND

Feeling empty? No Motivation? Joyless?

NEUROTRANSMITTER METABOLISM

Adapt or die. It's harsh, but true. As the saying goes, in life we can't always choose our circumstances. We can only choose how we respond and adapt to them. For many of us, difficult life events can shuttle us directly into painful emotional states – sadness, frustration, despair, even self-hate.

Grief is a classic example of how this works. When a loved one dies, we immediately go into a short period of shock. Then we crawl through a much longer period of sadness, anger, and longing. It's usually a long time before we are able to move on from these painful emotional states.

Other life stressors are less sudden, more drawn out. But that doesn't make them any less intense. These lingering stressors are more persistent, and often just as mentally and emotionally challenging. Financial difficulties, strained relationships, body image issues, all forms of oppression fall under this category of chronic life stressors.

These chronic life stressors are so hard on us because they can feel as if life is unfair, or something or someone is harming us, or that our destiny is just outside of our control. In facing such circumstances on a daily basis, we can easily get stuck in negative emotional states.

What happens when we live with the negative emotional states for too long? Those negative emotions then take on a life of their own. They change the way that we see the world, hear those around us, and even perceive ourselves. Stress that goes on too long can easily produce negativity shadows that follow us around. These negative emotional states that become our shadow are the seeds of shame, guilt, self-doubt, and later on mental illness.

So, we have to find a way to cope. The best coping style will vary from person to person. No one strategy is the absolute best. We just need to find a way out of those negative emotional states in which we can easily get stuck. If we can't find a way to cope, and these life problems persist, we will find ourselves swimming in negative emotional states day in and day out. Our human brains can handle a lot of stress. But there is a limit. The point in time when we reach that limit, is when mental illness symptoms are likely to emerge.

When faced with life stressors and these negative emotional states, seeing a therapist, speaking with a pastor, or reaching out to friends and family are good things to try (if available). A therapist, or our most therapeutic friend, can help us pause, step to the side, and see things from a different angle.

Just sitting with our thoughts can be transformative as well. Time spent reflecting moves the thoughts from a dark and doubtful place to a mindset that allows for more possibility. When we let it marinade for a while, we can begin to see our path to escape.

Even the mere passing of time can help. Time passing will help the pain fade. With time, we turn around, look back, and realize that magically somehow the pain has left us. Or rather, the pain stayed in place, and we moved on. Either way, time creates space between us and those negative emotional states. This time and space helps us respond to our problems in a much more constructive way.

All of these approaches – friends, therapy, spirituality, self-reflection, and even time – can help. What they all have in common is that each involves movement.

Initially when we are experiencing negative emotions like sadness, despair, fear, worry, or anger, we are glued to the pain. There's nothing else on our minds. We are breathing it in. There is little to no space between it and us. That's obviously not the ideal situation for us.

When we talk it out, sit and reflect, or allow time to heal us, the pain forces movement in our minds. Our thoughts move. Our feelings move. Even our memories move. These coping strategies create a wedge between us and the pain. They move us away from the negative emotional state that first accompanies the difficult circumstances. They move us out of negative into neutral acceptance of what is. They move us towards options, possibilities, and a life that's a much better fit for us.

How we respond to life is what matters most. Life is stressful, and we are emotional beings. That's a recipe for discontent, discomfort, and drama. Can you name one reality TV show that didn't capitalize on these two ingredients?

Life will unfold, and as it does, it usually finds a way to push our buttons. Something happens. We feel something. We respond. Our actions are usually influenced by what we are feeling at the moment. If we're angry, we lash out – and feel super justified in doing so. If we're sad or anxious, we retreat. The point is that life stress can steer us down the path towards those negative emotional states. Staying mentally and emotionally well is about course correcting.

So how do we do that? Well, in our efforts towards achieving mental wellness, our feelings will actually be useful. They are the guideposts along the way. When something bad happens, we typically feel bad. Once we get to feeling negative, that's when things can take a left turn. We have to be careful. A negative emotional state won't always tell us the truth. Instead it may just tell us something that selfishly makes its existence seem real and justified. This is why the words we utter in anger feel like the truest thing we've ever said aloud. That would be a sign we're headed in the wrong direction.

Yet, if we listen to these feelings in a certain way, they will help guide us in the right direction. Rather than immediately going with negative emotional states when they arise, it's clearly better to take a beat, be curious, and ask some "why" questions. When we reflect on why we feel certain negative emotional states, that then gives us the freedom to choose a different direction for the future. Often that means avoiding certain people or places, setting stronger boundaries with those we can't avoid, and finding people and situations that are a much better match for us. Listening to our feelings, accepting them, and heeding their wisdom aids us in making tough but important decisions.

When we acknowledge what we are feeling, then deciding against going down the direction that led us to the negative emotional state in the first place is much easier. We need emotional responses to help guide our choices in life. They are our teacher.

In summary, we cannot choose our fates. We can only choose how we respond. And the best response to any stressor is movement. A negative, limiting, and destructive emotional state can keep us stuck in place. Negative, limiting, and destructive emotional states fuel a similarly negative, limiting, and destructive thought pattern. A negative, limiting, destructive thought pattern in turn will dictate our actions and choices in life – often leading us to react in ways that recreate those initial negative, limiting, and destructive emotional states. Negative emotional states are greedy and selfish. They want to be felt all the time. They want you to feed on what they put in front of you. They want you to pay attention to them and nothing else. If we comply, we're stuck.

The best response is to break up the concrete and allow your thoughts and feelings the space to move around a bit. When we step back and get that outside perspective, we can see possibilities.

When we step out of negative emotional states, we can then choose a different option. That's the difference between reacting and responding. Reacting is going on pure emotions. Responding is a combination of emotion, space, time, reflection, and deciding.

FIRST RESPONDERS

In life, stuff happens. And, then we experience a response to whatever just happened. It takes a moment to be fully processed and produce a feeling, trigger a memory, or create a thought pattern. What's the link between things happening around us and our response?

Neurotransmitters! They are the first responders on the scene. They are the bridge between stuff happening around us and our internal mental and emotional reactions. However, neurotransmitters can also help us respond in ways that bring us peace and personal growth. It all depends on where, how much, and how active neurotransmitters are in our brains. As you'll learn, deficits of certain neurotransmitters tend to make us more reactionary and emotional. Adequate supply and activity of neurotransmitters tend to help us respond in ways that are healthier and more productive.

Let's dig a little deeper to see how all of this works inside the brain. Just like we want our emotions to move in order to create change in our lives, neurotransmitters actually move from one spot to another to make change happen in the brain. Our brains' response to life occurs because of movement. Neurotransmission is that movement. The movement is both chemical and electrical.

The chemical part is the array of neurotransmitters that circulate and act on neurons in the brain. There are over a hundred different kinds of neurotransmitters, but there's a small collection of key neurotransmitters that help manage our mental and emotional responses to life. You have likely heard of the popular ones... serotonin, dopamine, norepinephrine. What they all share in common is that they move. Neurotransmitters jump from one neuron to the next.

Once a neurotransmitter docks with a receiving neuron, then the electrical part happens. Once enough neurotransmitters float across and activate a receiving neuron, there is an electrical change that occurs inside that neuron. The electrical change then moves down the length of that neuron. The message eventually reaches the end terminal of that neuron. Once the electrical message reaches the end terminal, another electrical change occur which triggers the release of neurotransmitters from that neuron. As you may have guessed, those neurotransmitters then float across to the next neuron, and the cycle continues.

The chemical and electrical activity is all about movement. With all that movement, our brain is responding to life that is happening around us and even from within. It makes sense then, that neurotransmitters have been a central focus of mental health treatment for several decades.[115-117] Despite their critical importance, they're not the be all-end all of mental health treatment. There are days when us prescribers wish that were so. Our jobs would be easy. If all it took to get people better was adjusting neurotransmitter levels and function, then it would literally only take one visit. In reality, it's not that easy. Many other factors come into play.

Yet, finding ways to leverage control over neurotransmitter activity does impact our emotional lives and can definitely help. Adjusting the levels and activity of neurotransmitters with medication does lead to significant changes in how we experience life. Serotonin, dopamine, norepinephrine are the neurotransmitters commonly targeted with medications. Manipulating them with psychiatric medications does alter mood.[118-119]

In this chapter we will cover how neurotransmitters mediate our response to life. The remaining chapters will cover the other brain structures and functions that shape how we think and feel.

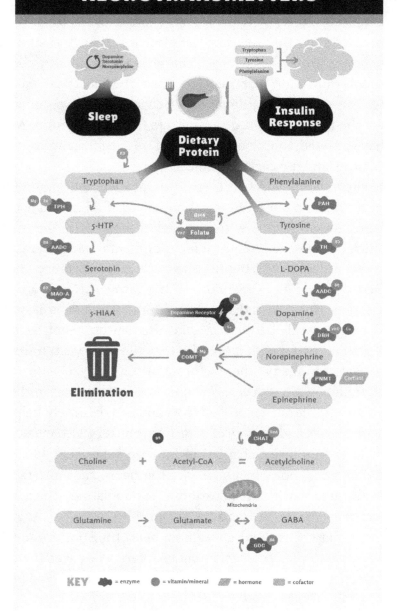

• *Sleep helps regenerate key neurotransmitters.*

• *Dietary protein is important for delivering tryptophan, tyrosine, and phenylalanine, and other amino acids to the brain for the creation of neurotransmitters.*

• *Insulin responses after meals help shuttle these amino acids that are the raw materials for serotonin, dopamine, and norepinephrine.*

• *Manufacture of neurotransmitters depends on fully functional enzymes (seen in dark green... TPH, AADC, PAH, TH, DBH), and these enzymes need specific vitamins and minerals to function.*

• *Once neurotransmitters are made and have done their job, they need to be degraded – there are enzymes for that as well (MAO-A, COMT), which also need specific vitamins and minerals to function.*

• *Receptors for neurotransmitters also need specific minerals to function optimally (Zinc and Selenium for Dopamine receptors).*

References: 132-158

LETTUCE ANSWER THE QUESTION

What happens to our brain chemistry if we eat poorly?

Take a look at the diagram above. Notice how neurotransmitter creation begins with adequate sleep and protein intake from our daily diet. Along the neurotransmitter production assembly line, key vitamins and minerals help speed up neurotransmitter production at specific spots. Finally, effective use and appropriate breakdown of neurotransmitters is supported by yet more vitamins and minerals.

Neurotransmitters are made up of amino acids that we obtain through consuming dietary proteins.[120] On the most practical level, we need to take in an adequate amount of protein to have enough amino acids to produce enough neurotransmitters.[121] Neurotransmitters can't do their job in the brain if they are in short supply.

For example, in a few studies where researchers depleted the amino acid tryptophan (raw material for serotonin) subjects immediately experienced depressed mood states.[122] Similarly, depletion of tyrosine and phenylalanine (raw material for dopamine) produced a decrease in motivation, reward seeking, and risk taking.[123] Now you can see how nutrition plays such an important role in neurotransmitter creation and function.

CIRCUIT TRAINING

It's important to have a healthy supply of neurotransmitters at the ready – not too little, not too much. But, maintaining the right 'levels' of neurotransmitters is not the whole story. There's more to the discussion of neurotransmitters than just the total amount someone has in their brain. It's similar to your bank account. Having a lot of money, or a little, or even a negative amount, does not always dictate how you spend money. How you spend money is based on many factors, not just on the dollar amount.

If we want to dig a little deeper into how these neurotransmitters mediate our response to life, let's pick up where we left off in the explanation of how neurotransmission works.

To review, for the brain to respond to life happening around us, neurons need to talk to one another. One neuron sends a message, another neuron receives the message, and then passes it along to the next. Each neuron continues to pass along the message to another nearby neuron. It happens in rapid succession, from one part of the brain to the other at incredible speed. This message sending and receiving in the brain is called neurotransmission. It's chemical, then electrical, then chemical again.

Again, neurotransmitters are the chemicals. They are stored in tiny sacs in the end terminals of neurons. They sit and wait for the electrical signal to come down the pipe. Once the electrical signal travels down the neuron and hits the end terminal, the neurotransmitter immediately release into the tiny space between two nearby neurons. This tiny space is called the synapse. The neurotransmitters float across that synapse and snuggle into receptors on a nearby neuron. If enough receptors on that nearby neuron are activated by enough neurotransmitters, then the same electrical message is passed along down that next neuron.[124]

This last part is important. Just one single neurotransmitter floating across and docking with a receptor on another neuron won't be nearly enough to get the job done. There needs to be a whole gaggle of neurotransmitters squirting out across the synapse and docking with the receiving neuron's receptors. It takes a certain number of neurotransmitters floating across and hitting receptors to meet threshold for an electrical change in the receiving neuron. Once that threshold is met, the electrical signal shoots down the length of that neuron, eventually leading to release of neurotransmitters at the other end.

A key player in this process of neurotransmission is the axon. The axon is the long spine of the neuron that gives neurons their length. It carries the electrical message from the receptors on one side of the neuron down to its end terminal on the other side. The electrical signal travels down the axon and finally reaches the end terminal. That electrical signal coming into the end terminal then triggers the end terminal to release neurotransmitters into the synaptic space between itself and another nearby neuron. This is how the message jumps from one neuron to the next.

In case your eyes just glazed over, or I just put you to sleep, let's make this more interactive. To get a better sense of what's happening, try this:

Hold your arms up in the air, forearms parallel with the ground. Fists should be pointed at one another, about to pound, but not quite touching. This is how neurons exist in the brain, close but not touching. That space in between the fists is called the synapse.

Now, imagine an electrical message travelling from your left elbow, down your forearm (the axon), all the way to the end of your left fist (end terminal). Once that electrical message reaches your fist, it triggers the release of a bunch of chemicals (neurotransmitters) that float across that tiny space between your fists (the synapse). Those chemicals have to dock with your right fist (receptors on the receiving neuron). If enough neurotransmitters dock with enough receptors on your right fist, it creates an electrical change and then the electrical message can continue down your right forearm – all the way down to your right elbow. Then the cycle will continue with another neuron (or imaginary arm on the other side of your right elbow).

Now, add up a massive series of neurons connected to one another and you have a brain circuit. The message continues from one neuron to the next in this electrical-chemical- electrical fashion. When a message travels the entire circuit (a massive number of neurons linked together across the brain), the brain then recognizes the pattern and we experience the memory, thought, feeling, sensation, or perception.[125] In the brain, these circuits loop around from one part of the brain to another and back again.[126-127]

The circuits represent many connections between neurons, from one part of our brain to another. Every memory, thought, feeling, sensation, or perception is a unique pattern of activation across a specific circuit. Each of these experiences is actually a distinctive lightning bolt signature that starts in one part of the brain, travels across to some other part.[125]

Here's another analogy to help explain what's happening. Think about the Maps app on your smartphone. It's easy. You type in a destination. The destination pops up and so does a big bold blue line from your location to the destination. Looks right, so you hit "go." The phone will show you the path you can take from wherever you are to that destination.

The electrical activity of the brain is similar. Circuits are jagged lightning bolt-like pathways that weave themselves across the brain. Each circuit is unique. Just like the zig zag blue line from your house to various destinations around town will be different.

In the Maps app, the route requires that you start out on one street, then connect to another street, and another, and so on until your get to your destination. In the brain, the circuits that represent memories, thoughts, feelings, sensation, and perceptions are a unique series of neurons connected to each other. Each thought, feeling, memory, sensation, or perception we experience is a unique signature.

In real life, it happens really fast. We are presented with an external or internal stimulus – a familiar face, a memory from long ago, a new experience, or some stimulus that produces a strong emotion – and a specific circuit is activated. Each specific memory is a unique pathway, or collection of neurons.

Going further with the Maps analogy, you can think of neurotransmitters, and their activity in between neurons, as the stoplights that connect one street to another (or one neuron to another). They act as the gates that help decide if the message continues through or will be stopped in its tracks.

Neurotransmitters are the lynchpin of brain activity. If the neurotransmitters aren't doing their job in between neurons, then the circuit won't be fully activated. If a circuit isn't fully activated when it needs to be, either nothing will happen or some less desirable alternative will happen.

In the study listed above, when scientists artificially lowered the amount of available dopamine in subjects, their behavior changed.[123] Once the dopamine was reduced, the subjects in the study appeared less motivated to take risks in order to obtain a reward. That was a noticeable difference in their responses compared to how they responded before the experiment. Action was replaced with apathy. Not surprisingly, there are other studies that show neurotransmitter depletion can lead to the onset of immediate mental illness symptoms.[121-122] Although this effect is generally seen in subjects who have previously experienced mental illness before the nutrient depletion.

This is why all the psychiatric medications we have act on some part of the synapse, either by pretending to be neurotransmitters, interacting with neurotransmitter receptors (both blocking activity or stimulating activity), or trying to adjust the availability of neurotransmitters in the synapse.

CHEMICALS IN BALANCE

It's a good idea to have a sufficient number of neurotransmitters available while we are working our way through life. The goldilocks principle applies here. Without ample neurotransmitters promoting free-flowing messages in the brain, certain functions would suffer. The ability to think through our emotions is one such function of the front part of the brain (prefrontal cortex) that protects us from depression and anxiety.[128] That function depends on serotonin,[129] dopamine,[130] and other neurotransmitters[131] passing along messages.

There can also be too much of a good thing. For example, the field of psychiatry believes that psychosis is brought about, in part, by an overactive circuit that uses dopamine. Psychosis is a condition where a person loses touch with reality. Common symptoms include hallucinations, paranoia, and delusions. The idea that psychosis was primarily driven by excess dopamine stemmed from the fact that medications that block dopamine from interacting with receptors (and thus preventing that circuit from running too hot) work relatively well at stopping psychosis.

Nature likely invented specific enzymes in the brain that help break down and eliminate neurotransmitters, because it can be equally harmful to have an excess availability of neurotransmitters as having a deficit.

Within the concept of neurotransmission, the theme of balance emerges as it does with most everything in nature. There's a delicate balance between production and destruction. More is not always better. That's only true at Costco. Balance is best. There are a host of vitamins, minerals, and other nutrients that come together to ensure that our brains adequately create neurotransmitters. Some of those same nutrients, along with a few others, are also needed to break down and eliminate neurotransmitters.

Our task is to create enough of a space in our hearts and minds to be able to sit down and figure out what is real and true. Our raw and immediate emotions often lie to us. They don't tell us the truth, or at least the full truth. They tell us a story that helps these emotions make sense. Only when we get a good handle on what's true and what's possible, can we have enough confidence and courage to make change happen. Finding the truth is important. It offers us peace and a better path forward.

In conclusion, we need neurotransmitters. We need an adequate supply of neurotransmitters to best respond to life. We need them to be available for use, then we need them to go away. We also need the biochemical mechanisms that manage their creation, activity, and elimination to be in good functioning order.

When all of this is in place, we then have the energy and resources to do the difficult job of responding to life's challenges with patience, poise, and curiosity. We can then find new and important meaning in life's difficulties and tragedies. Feed your brain so your neurotransmitters will be there to help you along the way.

Recommendation:

To achieve this balance, we need to give our brain enough raw materials – amino acids, vitamins, minerals, & other key nutrients. In addition, our brains need the right kinds of stimulation and challenge. Here's the take home... all you have to do is feed your brain the nutrients it needs, give it the right amount and kinds of stimulation, and your brain will take it from there.

To get started, focus on the basics – good sleep, adequate protein, and steady blood glucose levels. Generally, this means you should aim to sleep 7-8 hours a night. Do your best to eat three balanced meals every day. Animal meat is the best source of those vital amino acids, but you don't need to wolf down three steaks a day. Just make sure you're getting at least 1-2 palm-sized servings of animal meats a day. Also, eating breakfast is vital for brain function. Skipping breakfast means your brain has to do its best without an adequate supply of key nutrients and it adds way more stress to your system than you need.

All of these steps sound so simple but think about it. Can you say that you are doing all of the above every day?

Beyond those basic steps, consider eating red meat and liver for iron, B vitamins, and key fat- soluble vitamins. Fish and seafood also provide important fat-soluble vitamins, as well as Omega-3's, B12, and needed minerals. A variety of vegetables and beans also supply necessary B vitamins. Nuts and seeds offer neurotransmitter-boosting minerals, like magnesium, zinc, and selenium. Of course, don't forget about the value of fruit for Vitamin C.

Neurotransmitter Nutrients

Vitamin	Function	Food Sources
Vitamin A	Improves neurotransmitter signaling	liver, sweet potatoes, carrots, cantaloupe, red peppers, mangoes, black-eyed peas, apricots, cheese, eggs, salmon
Vitamin D	Turns on gene that creates serotonin	salmon, swordfish, trout, mackerel, herring, mushrooms, cheese, milk
Vitamin B3	Supports enzyme that creates dopamine	sunflower seeds, almonds, turnip greens, apricots, spinach, dandelion greens, swiss chard, red peppers, avocado, eggs, asparagus, herring, sardines, tuna

Vitamin B5	Raw material for creation of acetylcholine	mushrooms, parsley, spirulina, chives, sundried tomatoes, radish, pasilla peppers, avocados, apricots, dates, eggs, liver, beef, chicken, pork
Vitamin B6	Supports enzyme that creates serotonin, dopamine, & GABA	pasilla peppers, red peppers, chives, shallots, onions, parsley, garlic, leeks, prunes, apricots, bananas, eggs, cheese, tuna, salmon
Folate	Supports enzyme that creates serotonin, dopamine, & GABA	mussels, crab, salmon, eggs, cheese, chicken, leeks, edamame, radish, peppers, seaweed, parsley, asparagus, pasilla peppers, black-eyed peas, onions, leafy greens, Brussels sprouts, artichokes, broccoli, beets, chives, avocados, plantains, mangoes, oranges, pomegranates, blackberries, kiwi
Vitamin B12	Supports enzyme that creates serotonin & dopamine; Recycles Folate	clams, octopus, oysters, mackerel, salmon, fish roe, crab, tuna, eggs, cod

Vitamin C	Supports enzyme that breaks down dopamine into norepinephrine; Supports enzyme that regenerates serotonin & dopamine	kale, kiwi, oranges, watercress, broccoli, lemon juice, grapefruit, mango, garlic, spinach

Mineral	Function	Food Sources
Iron	Supports enzyme that creates serotonin & dopamine	(Heme) clams, oysters, mussels, beef, turkey, chicken (Non-Heme) lentils, chickpeas, black-eyed peas, kidney beans, white beans, black beans, potatoes with skin, raisins, apricots, cashews, almonds, pistachios, tahini, spirulina

Magnesium	Supports enzyme that creates dopamine; Supports enzyme that breaks down dopamine & norepinephrine	pumpkin seeds, almonds, peanuts, sunflower seeds, lima beans, plantains, potatoes, black-eyed peas, apricots, edamame, acorn squash, mussels, shrimp, clams, oysters, summer squash, tomatoes, milk, cheese, blackberries, arugula, dark chocolate (70% or greater)
Zinc	Improves function of dopamine receptors; Supports enzyme that creates dopamine	oysters, beef, pumpkin seeds, lobster, lamb, pasilla peppers, edamame, garlic, chickpeas, black-eyed peas, pinto beans, broccoli raab, mushrooms, fish, dark chocolate
Copper	Supports enzyme that breaks down dopamine into norepinephrine;	oysters, sunflower seeds, dark chocolate, almonds, apricots, crab, octopus, lobster, tuna
Selenium	Improves function of dopamine receptors	sunflower seeds, oysters, pumpkin seeds, halibut, swordfish, tuna, lobster, fish roe, fish, pork, chicken, turkey, brazil nuts = 544mcg per ounce

Amino Acid	Function	Food Sources
Tryptophan	Raw material for serotonin creation	(turkey, chicken, milk, cheese, tuna, peanuts, oats, banana
Tyrosine	Raw material for dopamine and norepinephrine creation	cheese, edamame, beef, lamb, pork, salmon, tuna, mackerel, shrimp, halibut, chicken, turkey, pumpkin seeds, eggs, beans, lentils, wild rice, spirulina
Phenylalanine	Raw material for dopamine and norepinephrine creation	beef, pork, chicken, eggs, cheese, nuts, beans, parsley, onion, potatoes, peas, okra, kale, green beans, spirulina
Methionine	Supports enzyme that regenerates serotonin	eggs, cod, spirulina, brazil nuts, beef, milk, lamb, cheese, turkey, chicken, pork, fish, edamame

~ 7 ~

BUILD

Memory Failing? Thinking Slowed Down? Ups & Downs?

HEALTHY CELL MEMBRANES:

If you have a family, or are in a relationship, or even if you have ever attempted to cancel your cable television service, you understand the importance of the message being received clearly, the first time. Communication in and across the brain is no different. As described in Chapter 5, neurons are the brain cells that do all the message sending and receiving.

To review, the axon is the long part of the neuron that carries the electrical message. Once the message reaches the end terminal, the release of chemical messengers called neurotransmitters is triggered. It's essential that the message reaches the end terminal so neurotransmission can continue.

The axon gives the neuron its length. Some neuronal axons can stretch up to multiple feet inside the body. For a message to successfully reach the end terminal, it must travel all the way down the axon. If the structure of the neuron is not optimal, messages can be lost or take too long to get to their destination.[159]

The axon also plays this super important role of protecting the integrity of the message while pushing it along from one end of the neuron to the other. Lost messages equal fuzzy thinking, memory lapses, and poor focus. Optimal communication depends upon optimal structure of neurons across the brain. And, optimal structure depends upon optimal nutrition.

THE GAME OF TELEPHONE

Our brains contain billions of neurons. Moreover, there's trillions of interconnections between all those billion neurons. Remember from the last chapter how it's a fully activated circuit in the brain that allows us to experience a thought, feeling, memory, sensation, or perception? For a neuronal circuit to be fully activated, communication between all the neurons in that circuit must happen fast and without mistakes or lost messages. Slow or interrupted messages allow more opportunity for miscommunication. If signals are lost, communication within the brain suffers.

It's like your conversation with the cable television sales representative. You call to cancel your service and after waiting an unnecessarily long time on hold, the representative answers and asks you a series of questions about yourself that feel both invasive and beside the point. Finally, it's your turn, and you state clearly that you want to cancel service. Instead of hearing your desire to cancel, the representative initiates the "customer retention" script. You try again. But the representative on the other end skips right past your deep yearning desire to cancel and goes on to tell you about the brand new, limited-time, very special promotional upgrade that just became available.

It would be much better if he or she heard you the first time. You sent your message loud and clear, but the message was lost. Frustration, confusion, and anxiety ensue. The brain can become similarly unsettled if messages from one area of the brain take too long to get through or somehow get lost along the way.

WHAT ARE YOU, THICK IN THE HEAD?

My grandfather, the "jiddo" to my sitto, loved to point out other people's foolish mistakes. It was one of his favorite pastimes. I'd always overhear him talking with my dad and uncles, and he'd often comment that so-and-so must be "thick in the head". As a kid, fear of being on the wrong end of this deep burn led me to spend a good amount of time in front of the mirror, trying to find which angle made my head look the thinnest. It was years later, after much scientific research, I discovered that being thick in the head was actually a good thing!

In her infinite wisdom, nature invented the myelin sheath to reduce the chances of lost messages in the brain and the associated communication problems that come with lost messages. Myelin is the name of chunks of fat that surrounds the axon of most neurons. This fatty layer actually increases the speed and efficiency of the electrical messages traveling down the axon.[159]

Let's continue with the cable theme to help explain the purpose, structure, and function of myelin. Picture in your mind the coaxial cables we use for our cable boxes and televisions. If you look at the end of the cable, you'll notice that in the center is a thin, copper-colored wire. It makes up a small part of the entire cable, but that copper part in the center does all the work of sending messages. The remaining diameter of the coaxial cable is a bunch of fuzzy insulation with a rubber coating on the outside. The insulation does not send the message, it's just there to protect against the signal floating away. It keeps the signal on track. Covering up the thin copper wire with insulation and rubber coating helps ensure that the signal is not lost on the way from the utility poles outside your house to your television.

NEURON ANATOMY

Receives messages

Dendrites

Sends messages

End Terminal

Axon

Myelin Sheath

On most neurons, it is the myelin sheath that provides insulation. Myelin is like that fuzzy insulation and rubber coating. The neuron itself is like the copper wire doing the transmitting of messages.

Despite seeming to play just a supportive role, myelin is actually really important for rapid and effective communication in the brain. The myelin sheath not only protects the integrity of messages by preventing the signal from dissipating before reaching its destination, it also boosts the speed by a hundred-fold.[159]

As you may have guessed, there are specific nutrients the brain requires to manufacture and install myelin along the axons. There's actually a specific breed of brain cells, called oligodendrocytes, that performs that job.[160] Oligodendrocytes require a host of nutrients from TMWD to manufacture and install myelin. But, myelin itself is made up of fatty substances, one of which is (brace yourself) cholesterol.[161] Yes, there is literally something positive about cholesterol. It is not the devil's spawn after all.

LOOK MA, NO HANDS!

So far we've made the case for speed and integrity (keeping messages on track and not losing them) as two key factors for optimal communication in the brain. Flexibility is a third essential quality that neurons must possess to be able to maintain optimal communication. Neurons, just like humans, need to be flexible. Being able to change where they move to, who they talk to, and how they respond to a changing environment is crucial for successful communication and learning in life.[162]

Those brain circuits discussed in the last chapter don't just come pre-set. Brain circuits become established through repetitive activity. As the saying in neurology goes, "neurons that fire together, wire together". Repeated chemical and electrical interaction between two neurons solidifies their connection. If they talk to each other a lot, they become friends and then move towards each other so they can easily interact with each other again in the future. But, just as it goes with some friends, their connection is not set in stone. Without repeated interaction or activity between them, the connection can weaken. All of this is called plasticity.

You have experienced plasticity. Do something once and it's awkward. Do it twice and it's somewhat familiar. Do it a hundred times and it's automatic. That is the brain using plasticity to learn and master new skills. Every new skill, including coping skills, become easier and more automatic the more we practice. It's similar to learning how to ride a bike.

Learning in life is the process of brain plasticity – the branching over and fusing together of neurons to form neuronal connections that make up circuits. Repetitive life experience forces plasticity in the brain.

Every time we learn something new, experience a novel sensation, or process an emotion, it molds and shapes the connections in our brain. Once these connections are established within our brains' vast network of neurons, we become more automatic with our thoughts, feelings, and behaviors. This automatic responding can be good for us or bad for us. Once we learn to ride a bike, we can effortlessly cruise around, daydream, and enjoy ourselves. We don't have to put effort into focusing on pedaling, balancing, braking. It's automatic.

However, automatic responses can also lead us astray. Rather than perceiving things in a neutral, unbiased way, our automatic negative thoughts can jump in and color the situation in an unrealistic, negative way. In the therapy world, this concept of automatic negative thoughts is very popular. In life, stuff happens, and it leaves a mark. Ever found yourself over-reacting to something someone said, or the way that they say it, or even the way their face looked? Certainly, there's something about that that triggered you. It's probably something that happened in the past and it's unresolved. Or, maybe it was just plain rude. Whatever the case, a simple hand gesture, facial expression, or tone sends you on a bullet train to feeling something strong and negative – anger, disappointment, fear, self-consciousness, guilt, shame... the list is long.

It happens quick, too quick to realize what happened. And that's the point. Our brains start out like a dense, lush forest. Neurons growing everywhere, no real organization. Then life proceeds and we start wearing in pathways across the forest (or brain). By the time we are adults we have well-worn paths crisscrossing our brains. How long would it take you to trample across an untouched forest? How long would it take you to get to the other side of the forest if you took the well-worn path?

Sometimes, we need to make a new path, one that's just as well-worn. This is the process therapists take with their patients. They try to reframe situations, get patients to see things from a different angle, and hope that they then take a different path in the future. Speed, integrity, and flexibility are three key aspects of plasticity.

Ensuring that your brain's neurons possess those ingredients will only support that kind of positive change.

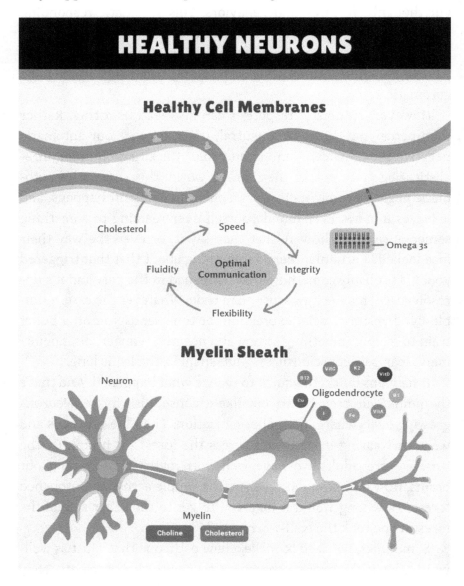

• *Cholesterol is an essential part of neuronal membranes. It keeps the membrane intact and durable yet fluid and responsive to communication.*

• *Omega-3 fatty acids are also embedded in the neuronal membranes, and they provide flexibility which aids plasticity in the brain.*

• *Oligodendrocytes are cells that are responsible for building myelin on neuronal axons. Oligodendrocytes utilize a number of vitamins, minerals, and other nutrients to lay down healthy and functional myelin.*

Plasticity offers us the potential to improve our mental wellness. With active and adaptive plasticity, things start to come together. What was once confusing, bewildering, and seemingly out of our control, now begins to make more sense. We can now see what's happening, when it's happening. Plasticity helps connect the dots between our experiences and our reactions to those experiences. It helps explain why we are feeling whatever it is we are feeling at that moment. This consolidation of experiences and emotions leads to greater skill and wisdom.[163]

If you think about it, wisdom is often the antidote to mental illness symptoms. Wisdom is what we search for when we peruse the self-help aisle of the bookstore. Wisdom is what we seek when we see a therapist or consult a pastor. Wisdom gets us through really challenging times with poise and grace.

GO WITH THE FLOW

Let's review. We need signal speed and integrity to keep the messages flowing correctly. To connect all the dots in our lives, we need flexibility. For optimal communication, we need one more element: fluidity.

Fluidity means that the outer cell membranes of neurons can bend, twist, and adapt the local chemical, electrical, and structural environment. the brain needs the neuronal cell membranes to be fluid in order to respond to ever-changing circumstances that life throws our way.[164-167]

Fluidity allows protein transporters to embed inside the neuronal membranes. Protein transporters and receptors allow neurotransmitters, peptides, hormones, and other substances to interact with neurons. They are the ears of the neurons and they hear what messages the body and brain are trying to send.

Speed, integrity, flexibility, and fluidity all keep our neurons healthy and functional— exactly what we need to be flexible, balanced, and sharp in our daily lives.

Recommendation:

What's the secret to healthy thick myelin, flexible neurons, and fluid neuronal cell membranes? Fatty foods with a side of veggies!

Now don't freak out. It's true that many fatty foods are clearly toxic. These would be the processed foods that are loaded with trans fats. What I'm recommending here are the foods that provide healthy fats, such as olive oil, coconut oil, wild fish, grass-fed animal meats, eggs, nuts, seeds, and dairy for those who can tolerate it.

Choline and cholesterol are two key raw materials oligodendrocytes use to produce myelin. Both choline and cholesterol can easily be obtained through these healthy fatty foods. Look to egg yolks, seafood, nuts and seeds to stock up.

To support your oligodendrocytes in making myelin, you need a host of vitamins and minerals (Vitamins B12 & B1, Vitamin C, Vitamin K2, Vitamin D, Vitamin A, Iron, Iodine, & Copper).[160] A variety of plant foods, including vegetables, beans, nuts and seeds will offer you plenty of these vitamins and minerals. Animal meat is another important source of these vitamins and minerals. Don't forget to mix in some seaweed snacks for the iodine!

For fluid and flexible membranes, polyunsaturated omega-3 fatty acids, also known as Omega-3s, are super important. Omega 3s help keep the neuronal membranes flexible and fluid.[164-167] The unique shape of these particular fatty acids allows the outer membrane of the neuron to bend and adapt to its environment. This ability to bend and adapt facilitates optimal communication between neurons and overall plasticity in the brain, another good reason to consider adding more fish, seafood, and grass-fed red meat into your diet.

Cell Membrane Nutrients

Vitamin	Function	Food Sources
Vitamin A	Supports oligodendrocytes in creating myelin	liver, sweet potatoes, carrots, cantaloupe, red peppers, mangoes, black-eyed peas, apricots, cheese, eggs, salmon
Vitamin D	Supports oligodendrocytes in creating myelin	salmon, swordfish, trout, mackerel, herring, mushrooms, cheese, milk
Vitamin K2	Supports oligodendrocytes in creating myelin	cheese (pastured/grass-fed), eggs (yolks), pork, oysters, dark chicken, liver
Vitamin B1	Supports oligodendrocytes in creating myelin	tomatoes, edamame, peas, kidney beans, pinto beans, acorn squash, sunflower seeds, tahini, potatoes, milk, peppers, onions, garlic, asparagus, broccoli raab

		clams, octopus, oysters, mackerel, salmon, fish roe, crab, tuna, eggs, cod
Vitamin B12	Supports oligodendrocytes in creating myelin	clams, octopus, oysters, mackerel, salmon, fish roe, crab, tuna, eggs, cod
Vitamin C	Supports oligodendrocytes in creating myelin	kale, kiwi, oranges, watercress, broccoli, lemon juice, grapefruit, mango, garlic, spinach

Mineral	Function	Food Sources
Iodine	Supports oligodendrocytes in creating myelin	seaweed, cod, yogurt, milk, shrimp, eggs, tuna, prunes, cheese, lima beans *Iodized Salt = ¼ tsp = 71mcg *Nori Sheets = 1 gram = 15-40mcg
Iron	Supports oligodendrocytes in creating myelin	(Heme) clams, oysters, mussels, beef, turkey, chicken (Non-Heme) lentils, chickpeas, black-eyed peas, kidney beans, white beans, black beans, potatoes with skin, raisins, apricots, cashews, almonds, pistachios, tahini, spirulina
Copper	Supports oligodendrocytes in creating myelin	oysters, sunflower seeds, dark chocolate, almonds, apricots, crab, octopus, lobster, tuna

Nutrient	Function	Food Sources
Choline	Raw material for myelin creation	shiitake mushrooms, radish, sundried tomatoes, spirulina, cauliflower, potatoes, shallots, egg (yolks), milk, fish roe, shrimp, salmon, scallops, clams, cod, flaxseeds, pistachios, pumpkin seeds, cashews, sunflower seeds, pine nuts, almonds
Cholesterol	Raw material for myelin creation	eggs, liver, squid, chicken, oyster, lobster, crab, fish, pork, lamb, butter, beef, milk, cheese, yogurt
Omega 3's (DHA)	Raw material for cell membranes of neurons	fish roe, mackerel, salmon, swordfish, oyster, tuna, sardines

~ 8 ~

FUEL

Impulsive? Fatigued? Fussy?

FUNCTIONAL MITOCHONDRIA

Ever in a group and you put your foot in your mouth? Ever say something that sounded hilarious in your own mind, but turned out to be devastatingly offensive when spoken aloud?

It happens. You see something that's amazingly funny, and immediately comment. Sometimes you get that tickle in your mind, a tiny voice that tries to get you to hold back. It whispers, "if you say it, you'll regret it". But the impulse is strong, "say it, just say it... it's gonna be hilarious!". The impulse is not suppressed, and it goes terribly. Think about how much effort it takes to hold back. Think about those times when you had to bear down just to edit what you say into something more socially acceptable.

Our brains are capable of so many amazing feats. We tend to think of brain power in terms of all the impressive things the human brain can do. Whether it's math, memory, music, art, or people skills, each of us possess some pretty remarkable talents. The ability to not do something is not usually seen as a talent or skill. But how smart were you when you blurted out that super witty, but ultimately offensive comment? Sometimes, not doing something is the smartest move of all. Said another way, it requires a lot of energy to not freak out when there's stuff going on that makes us want to freak out. That's inhibition at work.

Our brains have to spend just as much effort and energy to not do something. How much willpower does it take not to go back to the cookie jar just one more time? In brain science terminology, that not doing something is called inhibition. Inhibition not only saves friendships, it helps us think clearly, stay productive, and find peace amidst the chaos of life. That's because inhibition is the check and balance on excitation in the brain. Our brains are pretty active. But if we were experiencing all that activity all at the same time, all the time, that would be nuts. We wouldn't be able to stay on any one thing and we'd be all over the place with our thoughts and emotions. Inhibition thus saves the day by muting a lot of brain activity so the brain can focus on one thing at a time. This creates order out of chaos.

DON'T JUST DO SOMETHING, SIT THERE

Inhibition is essential for existing as a fully functional and mentally balanced adult who practices socially acceptable behavior. The brain is really powerful and can easily get out of hand. Consider psychosis as an example. Truth be told, everyone has the capacity to become psychotic. We don't need a scientific journal article reference to know this is true. All you really need is LSD or magic mushrooms or a massive dose of dopamine boosting amphetamines.

We all have the machinery in our brains to experience psychosis (it's a brain circuit called the mesolimbic pathway). If you fuel those areas with enough chemical and electrical activity, you will definitely experience hallucinations and other forms of psychosis.

Unfortunately for many, psychosis occurs without the aid of hallucinogenic substances. Something else is going on that scientific researchers have not yet figured out. As with all mental illness, it's likely that genetics are involved. We all carry different levels of risk for each kind of illness. When we do become ill, it's because that risk (big or small) combined with environmental stressors (big or small) brings out the illness.

The point is that the capacity to experience mental illness lies within all of us. Some will be more easily triggered by stress than others. Some will face more stress than others. This is why depression, panic attacks, or even psychosis are neither a sign of weakness, nor a choice. It's just our genetic risk and our environmental stress working together.

We often think of psychosis as an extreme version of mental illness. In many ways it is. However, for all kinds of mental illness symptoms, we can find studies that use brain scans that reveal increased activity in certain areas, or between specific areas of the brain (circuits), in subjects with anxiety, depression, psychosis, and other disorders. This is where inhibition comes into play. Its purpose is to act as a stopgap for increased activity in any one particular circuit in the brain.

The takeaway here is that inhibition is generally an important thing for the brain. It serves to limit overactive circuits that can disrupt our mental and emotional experiences in life. Without inhibition constantly working in the background, life would be an emotional and behavioral "no rules" steel cage match.

POWER MOVES

So how do we get more inhibition going? How can we stop ourselves from telling our boss that he has a green thing in his teeth during a very important business lunch? In many respects, it boils down to energy. Our brain needs energy to be able to inhibit a thought, emotion, or behavior. It needs energy for inhibition just as it does for mental arithmetic. Doing and not doing are both energy-dependent processes.

How do we ensure our brains have enough energy? Well, there is no energy in our bodies without healthy, well- fed, active, vibrant mitochondria.

Let's cover what mitochondria are and how they are so important to brain function and mental wellness. Mitochondria suck up oxygen and glucose (they can also use the breakdown products of fat and protein). Once mitochondria take in enough oxygen and glucose, they spit out energy in the form of a little chemical battery called ATP.[180] This ATP fuels all cells and tissues in the body, including the brain.

Mitochondria are the reason we exist as we do today. We are no longer the legless, scaly sea creatures that crawled out of the sea millions of years ago. At some point, we borrowed mitochondria from bacteria, incorporated them into our cells, and then were able to evolve into upright, sentient beings with big, fat, juicy brains. It was the presence of mitochondria in our human cells that allowed our body to develop and our brains to grow bigger over time.

Without adequate energy, our bodies and brains would have chosen to conserve what energy they had, resisted the pressure to grow, and just slithered back into the sea. The brain takes up 20% of our energy supply on a daily basis.[181] There's a limit to how much glucose and oxygen any human can take in during a day, but mitochondria found a way to maximize the use of glucose and oxygen. In fact, the electron transport chain in mitochondria can extract 19 times as much energy as glycolysis, the junior varsity version of burning glucose for energy that doesn't produce big, fat, juicy brains.

Over the millennia of evolution, with more energy available, the human brain began to grow in size. Mitochondria offered the fuel needed to expand the size, thickness, and efficiency of the brain. One key area of growth during this time was the front part of the brain, also known as the frontal cortex.

The frontal cortex in humans is all about being smart and savvy. It's responsible for uniquely human capabilities such as problem-solving, thinking into the future, managing complex social interactions, and inhibiting emotional responses. With greater capacity to think, plan ahead, socialize, and strategize, humans were able to tackle greater challenges. And that's how we evolved into our brilliant and messy species we are today. The frontal cortex still helps us problem solve, process emotion, edit our behaviors, and socialize confidently. Nowadays, much of the research on emotional regulation, cognition, and behavioral control focuses on the frontal cortex.

GAS FOR YOUR BRAKE

So energy matters. Mitochondria offers our brains the bulk supply of energy. With adequate energy, our brain can do things. More importantly, with enough energy at the ready, our brain can stop us from doing things. At the outset, that doesn't seem that important. But we've covered a few examples of how being able to inhibit our speech is really valuable. In order to edit what we say before we say it, our frontal cortex has to be able to keep other parts in check. That requires energy.[182]

There's actually a smaller area within the frontal cortex, called the prefrontal cortex that puts the brakes on speech, but also behavior and emotion. The prefrontal cortex sits just behind your eyeballs. A critical job of the prefrontal cortex is to "modulate" or shush the other parts of the brain, especially the fear center.[183-184]

That's a pretty nice feature of the modern adult brain. Think about it. How do we react when we are afraid or worried? Something is wrong, you just know it. Fear wells up inside of you. In these moments, whatever fear bubbles up in your mind or spews out of your mouth is often the opposite of helpful and productive.

The hope is, in these red-hot moments, our prefrontal cortex kicks into gear and helps us see all the angles, not just the perspective that makes us throw a nutty. Especially when people are watching, it helps to play it cool. Yet, without an energized frontal cortex in good working order, we are liable to react on pure raw emotion. Alternatively, an energized, turned-on frontal cortex comforts us, "It's okay... it'll work out... I'll find a way".

The frontal cortex cannot adequately keep our red-hot emotions in check if it doesn't have enough energy to do so. For this, energy is key.[184] If you're succeeding at being a responsible, intelligent, reasonable adult, to some degree you have your mitochondria to thank. The energy produced by mitochondria is what fuels the brake pedal in your brain.

THE RIGHT STUFF

To be sure, there is an abundance of research on the importance of maintaining numerous healthy and functional mitochondria for overall health. There's also plenty of research supporting the role of healthy and functional mitochondria in ensuring mental & emotional wellness and optimal brain function.[185-186] The opposite effect has also borne out in the scientific research on mitochondria and mental health. Deficits in mitochondrial function and energy production are linked to every major mental illness.[186]

This makes sense, as mitochondria not only provide energy for brain function, but also to stave off oxidative stress and help every organ work at its best.[187] Without healthy mitochondria, our digestive systems would not absorb nutrients efficiently.[188] Our muscles wouldn't be the amazing metabolic reservoirs they can be.[188] Our livers would not be able to store and release needed nutrients on demand.[188] And, our prefrontal cortex would not be able to suppress some of the darker energy that lies dormant deep within in all of our human brains. It's there, swirling around, just waiting to be let out. The frontal cortex keeps those primal emotions under wraps by burying them under layers of rational thought.

Take a look at the diagram below to see how common nutrients play an essential role in mitochondrial energy production.

MITOCHONDRIAL HEALTH

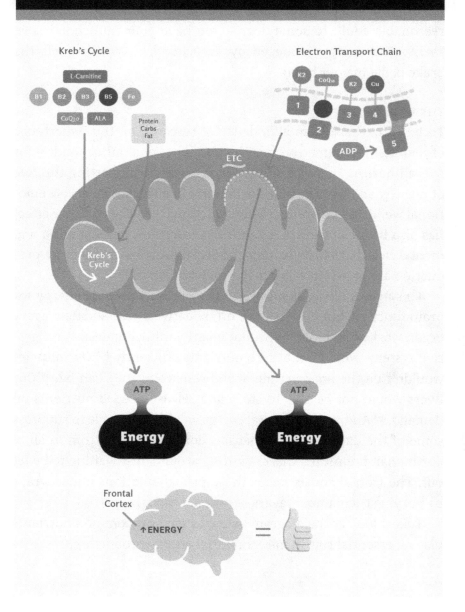

• *Glucose, fat, and protein can all act as the raw material for energy creation in mitochondria.*
• *The Kreb's cycle (Citric Acid cycle) uses vitamins and minerals to churn out ATP needed for a very energy dependent brain.*
• *Massive amounts of ATP are created down the line in the Electron Transport Chain of the mitochondria. For this, the mitochondria need Vitamin K2, Coenzyme Q10, and Copper.*

It may be easy to overlook the value of something that is so pervasive. Mitochondria are everywhere and no one place in particular at the same time. Mitochondria exist in every cell for a reason. Every cell needs energy. Every organ needs energy. The brain is no exception. You got something in your teeth.

Recommendation:

TMWD includes so many nutrients vital for optimally functioning mitochondria.

Mitochondria thrive on B vitamins, Coenzyme Q10, Vitamin K2, iron & copper for ATP production. Here again, animal foods are vitally important.

Remember that electron transport chain in the mitochondria which exponentially boosts ATP output? Well, that part of the mitochondria uses three critically important nutrients to get the job done: Vitamin K2, Coenzyme Q10, and Copper. This is another reason to focus on liver, grass-fed red meat, grass-fed dairy, fish, seafood, eggs, nuts and seeds.

L-carnitine is a key nutrient that helps shuttle fatty acids into mitochondria. With the aid of carnitine, these fatty acids can be used in the same way glucose is for ATP production. This function of carnitine boosts our energy supply, especially in the brain. This nutrient is almost exclusively found in meat, although one outlier is avocado.

Creatine is another key nutrient that offers our brain cells a quick and readily available energy supply. Creatine acts as a short-term energy source for neurons. This comes in super handy when ATP is still being replenished elsewhere in the mitochondria. Outside of bodybuilding supplement stores, you can also find this incredible nutrient in animal meat, dairy, eggs, and seafood.

As you can see, in TMWD meat is essential. Again, you don't need to take down three porterhouse steaks a day to get the benefits. Just make sure you give your body a chance to access the key nutrients your mitochondria need from your weekly diet. Simply eating red meat 3-4 times per week is enough. Same is likely true for fish, seafood, eggs, and dairy. In other words, a vegetarian meal here and there won't hurt you. In fact, it actually may be healthier than big portions of meat at every meal. Some is good. A lot may be okay, may not be okay. None is definitely no bueno for brain function. So, don't be afraid of meat. Be afraid of who you might become without feeding your brain these key nutrients.

Mitochondria Supporting Nutrients

Vitamin	Function	Food Sources
Vitamin K2	Supports production of ATP in mitochondria	cheese (pastured/grass-fed), eggs (yolks), pork, oysters, dark chicken, liver
Vitamin B1	Supports production of ATP in mitochondria	tomatoes, edamame, peas, kidney beans, pinto beans, acorn squash, sunflower seeds, tahini, potatoes, milk, peppers, onions, garlic, asparagus, broccoli raab
Vitamin B2	Supports production of ATP in mitochondria	almonds, blueberries, mushrooms, beans, black-eyed peas, kale, edamame, watercress, beet greens, spinach, asparagus, grapes, apricots, plantains, tahini

Vitamin B3	Supports production of ATP in mitochondria	peppers, potatoes, mushrooms, lentils, kidney beans, peas, sweet potatoes, apricots, blackberries, mangoes, plantains, oranges, beef, pork, chicken
Vitamin B5	Supports production of ATP in mitochondria	mushrooms, parsley, spirulina, chives, sundried tomatoes, radish, pasilla peppers, avocados, apricots, dates, eggs, liver, beef, chicken, pork
Coenzyme Q10	Supports production of ATP in mitochondria	liver, beef, EVOO, chicken, herring, tuna, edamame, butter, eggs, avocado, broccoli, cauliflower, cabbage, oysters, oranges, pistachios, walnuts, sesame seeds

Mineral	Function	Food Sources
Iron	Supports production of ATP in mitochondria	(Heme) clams, oysters, mussels, beef, turkey, chicken (Non-Heme) lentils, chickpeas, black-eyed peas, kidney beans, white beans, black beans, potatoes with skin, raisins, apricots, cashews, almonds, pistachios, tahini, spirulina
Copper	Supports production of ATP in mitochondria	oysters, sunflower seeds, dark chocolate, almonds, apricots, crab, octopus, lobster, tuna
Magnesium	Supports production of ATP in mitochondria	pumpkin seeds, almonds, peanuts, sunflower seeds, lima beans, plantains, potatoes, black-eyed peas, apricots, edamame, acorn squash, mussels, shrimp, clams, oysters, summer squash, tomatoes, milk, cheese, blackberries, arugula, dark chocolate (70% or greater)

Nutrient	Function	Food Sources
L-Carnitine	Shuttles fatty acids into mitochondria to boost ATP production	beef, pork, milk, cod, avocado *L-Carnitine biosynthesized in body from Lysine. Food Sources of Lysine: beef, chicken, pork, fish, milk, cheese, yogurt, eggs, apples, apricots, pears, avocados, pineapple, green beans, asparagus
Creatine	Provides short-term energy supply for neurons	beef, pork, milk, cheese, yogurt, eggs, mussels, clams, oysters
Alpha-lipoic Acid	Supports production of ATP in mitochondria	Coconut (provides precursor Caprylic Acid)

~ 9 ~

PROTECT

Brain Fog? Cranky? Racing Thoughts?

BALANCED IMMUNITY

Growing up with two older sisters was an incredible experience. It was incredible having two older sisters around every day to teach me things, protect me from dangers, and genuinely care for me. I wouldn't be who I am today without their support, wisdom, and shared laughter.

On another note, it was also incredible what these two got away with when my parents weren't around. They would dress me up in their clothes, paint my face with their makeup, make me fetch things for them, and were always coming up with hysterical practical jokes to play on me. Funny how those closest to you – the people who would do anything to protect you – are the ones who can also get your goat the most.

If you ask them today about all this, they might offer a subtle dismissal by noting that I'm "the sensitive type". They wouldn't be wrong. When I was young, life often felt hard. But through their program of character development, I learned to tolerate distress pretty well. What doesn't kill you, makes you stronger, right? How does this relate to the brain? Let's discuss...

So far, we have discussed neurons, and how they mediate our experiences in life. When we think of the brain, we envision a big tangled network of neurons. But neurons are not alone in the brain. In between and all around the neurons sit glial cells. They feed neurons, help neurons stay in place, keep the area around neurons clean, and as we discussed above, produce myelin to increase the efficiency of communication in the brain.

Glial cells are like the mortar holding all the bricks in a wall together. The bricks in a wall are what catch our eye. However, the mortar, which tends to fade into the background, is just as important. Without the mortar holding the wall together, there would just be a pile of bricks. Similarly, glial cells don't get as much attention as neurons, but they help keep all the neurons together and functional.

Microglia are a specific type of glial cell. Microglia are basically there to protect the neurons. You might not think that neurons are in much danger deep beneath skin and bones. Because the brain is so important to our functioning and survival, nature invented these watchmen just in case. Not only are they important. They are also numerous. Interestingly, in some brain areas, microglia outnumber neurons.[195]

Nature tends to be very conservative with its resources. The body would not be frivolous with spending resources to create and maintain certain brain cells if it was not worth it. If microglia outnumber neurons, it gives you an idea of how important they are to our health and function. What do they do? Microglia are not used for communication. Instead, they are there to protect the brain from infections, toxins, and other insults.[196-198]

Here's how it works...

Microglia take up the in-between spaces in the brain's interwoven network of neurons. They lie in wait, ready to serve when the brain is challenged by a toxin, dying cell, or infection. Before being called to action, microglia stay relatively dormant.

Certain toxins and microbes (bacteria and viruses) can find their way into the brain. Once they do, our loyal and dutiful microglia sense the invasion and spring into action. Microglia have a few weapons they use to fight back.

When a problem arises, they become "activated" and start spewing out chemicals or turn into Pacman-like globs that can eat up toxic substances in the area.[196] Once they are "activated," they will spray out inflammatory messengers called cytokines in the brain. The cytokines signal for other immune cells to migrate over and help.

FRIED NERVES

The problem is that they can be equally effective in protecting the brain as they can in destroying neurons and interrupting normal brain function. In some cases, it is the activated microglia that begin to harm the nearby neurons.

In the face of some toxin or infection, activated microglia are there help to us. However, in the context of excessive inflammation or environmental toxin exposure, microglia remain activated. They continue to spew out their own assaults (cytokines) even after the original toxin or infection was disarmed. With no real enemy to attack, activated microglia then turn their weaponry on nearby healthy neurons, killing them.[199] These neurons are innocent bystanders in an unnecessary war.

Before an infectious bug or toxic invader can get to the neurons, microglia step in to disarm and neutralize these threats. Then neurons can proceed as normal, blissfully unaware. Microglia take their job seriously. Unfortunately, sometimes too seriously. Just like my sisters, microglia make sure that no outsider ever comes enters the brain and messes with the neurons. If anyone is going to screw with the neurons, it's the microglia.

Microglia are here to protect us. If the defense is balanced, the microglia work to keep the brain clean by attacking the right targets, at the right time, in the right places, to the right degree. If our immune system is balanced, microglia are able to sense when the threat has passed. With help from those signals from the body that things are okay, microglia are able to turn off. They stop being activated.

So, with any kind of physical illness or imbalance in the body, there's an ever-present danger in too many microglia being activated unnecessarily, or certain microglia staying activated for too long.[200] If the protective response of microglia is too aggressive, then inflammation and neuronal destruction will ensue.

Excessive exposure to the toxic environmental stressors of modern-day life triggers our immune system to react (inflammation). Examples of these modern-day toxins and stressors include diets full of processed foods and sugar, lack of movement and exercise, poor quality air and water, exposure to industrial toxins and pollutants, and even mental and emotional stress. All of these environmental factors can lead our microglia to become chronically and unnecessarily over-activated.[200]

The most important thing to remember is this: When there is excessive inflammation in the brain, that can lead to excessive excitation. Excessive excitation is when our neuronal receptors are overstimulated.[201] When our neurons are overstimulated, we can begin to suffer from mental health symptoms.[6,83-85,202] We will cover more of this in the next chapter. For now, just know that too much excitation is bad for our mental wellness.

An inflamed brain can cause us to feel distracted, unmotivated, foggy, irritable, and like we want to recede inward. While not the sole cause, inflammation in the brain can definitely contribute to depressive and anxious symptoms.[6,83-85,202] In some cases, it can lead to more severe mental illness, such as schizophrenia.[203]

A THANKSGIVING TO REMEMBER

Here's something to remember... inflammation begets more inflammation. Once you start out down the path of toxicity, oxidative stress, and inflammation, it can become a runaway train. Inflammation can overstimulate and eventually destroy neurons. Once they die, cell fragments yard sale all over neighboring neurons. The mess has to be cleaned up swiftly and then the inflammatory reaction needs to stop. If it doesn't, that response can harm the brain.

It's just like that one Thanksgiving dinner where all it took was just that one comment from Auntie. Family members start chiming in, bringing up old stuff, taking it to a whole other level. A little flame turns into a house fire.

The job of the microglia is to clean up those dead or dying brain cells. It's an important job. But there's a delicate balance to be struck. Once those cells die and spill their guts all over the place, it gives the microglia and other immune cells in the brain another reason to stay active. Activated microglia, if unchecked and persist past the point of being helpful, can actually worsen the problem by killing more and more innocent neighboring brain cells by spewing out their inflammatory cytokines.[199-200]

This is like the other highlight of Thanksgiving when grandma offers to help do the dishes, but then ends up pulling out all your dishes and glassware in order to reorganize them in a way that "makes way more sense". What starts out helpful, can end up being less so.

Modern-day life can be toxic & inflammatory. Inflammation can overstimulate our brain, which can produce mental illness symptoms in the moment. What's worse is what can happen in the long run. Any neuron that gets overstimulated has the potential to give up and die. This overstimulation leading to neuronal cell death is called excitotoxicity.[204] The death of these brain cells can contribute to neurodegenerative diseases like Alzheimer's and Parkinson's Disease.

Of all the things to worry about, excessive inflammation in the brain should be one of them. Remember, the cascade of neuronal death continues until some other anti-inflammatory influence steps in and tones down the activated microglia.[205]

WHO WANTS PIE?

Fortunately, many of the nutrients highlighted in TMWD can help to tame overactive microglia. Plant foods actually play a bigger role here. Flavonoids are key nutrients that can help quell inflammation and activated microglia. Flavonoids are a subcategory of polyphenols. Curcumin from turmeric, resveratrol from grapes, and EGCG from green tea are some polyphenols you might recognize from TV commercials. Yet, in addition to these popular ones, there are a number of others with long, funny sounding names that can combat inflammation in the brain.

Flavonoids are actually the pigments in many colorful plant foods. Once they get into the brain, they provide that anti-inflammatory signal that can rebalance the immune system in the brain.

Flavonoids step in to protect innocent cells from being harmed by overactive microglia.[206] As mentioned, microglia step in when something seems off with a neuron. It may have been damaged by a toxin or infection. It may have been overstimulated to the point of exhaustion and then it gives up and decides to die. When something's off with neurons, microglia get work. They either eat up the dead and dying cell parts, or they marshal other immune cells to the area by churning out inflammatory cytokines. When microglia send out their cytokines, they are fighting fire with fire. Sometimes all that aggressive action creates more of a mess. [207]

Flavonoids arrive on the scene and they try to mop up some of the chaos – flavonoids are the medics to the microglial foot soldiers. Flavonoids offer aid to neurons by acting as antioxidants. Antioxidants are the heroes of the brain that jump in front of oxidative stress bullets. If effective, flavonoids save cells from harm, and from being overstimulated.[208]

BALANCED IMMUNITY

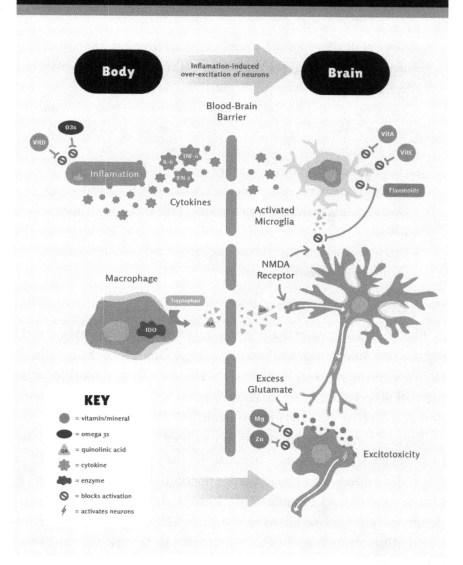

• *Vitamin D and Omega 3 fatty acids are critical for preventing inflammation in the body from getting out of control, which helps keep the brain's immune system in*
balance.

• *Cytokines (Il-6, TNF-alpha, IFN-gamma, among others) are the inflammatory messengers that can activate microglia in the body and overstimulate excitatory neurons in the brain.*

• *Quinolinic Acid is a byproduct of inflammation in the body that can also overstimulate excitatory neurons. Inside Macrophages, and enzyme called Indoleamine 2,3-dioxygenase (IDO) steals tryptophan and converts it into Quinolinic Acid, which then crosses into the brain.*

• *Vitamin A, Vitamin E, and Flavonoids are nutrients that can quell activated microglia, reducing the inflammatory (and excitatory) burden in the brain.*

• *Magnesium and Zinc are protective against inflammation induced overstimulation of excitatory neurons*

Flavonoids also calm the immune response in the brain by stunting the flow of excessive inflammatory cytokines from microglia.[208] Even more impressive, flavonoids act as signaling molecules that turn off activated microglia, returning microglia to their dormant, non-destructive state in times of health.[209-211]

Beyond flavonoids, there are some other familiar nutrients that help balance the immune response in the brain. Vitamin A[212] & E[213-214] dampen the activated microglial cytokine release. Omega-3s[215-216] and vitamin D[217-218] put a check on overactive inflammatory response all over the body. That's important, as inflammation originating in the body somewhere may have been the original problem that activated the previously dormant microglia.

These are all great nutrients to have on board as we face a highly inflammatory and toxic world. Maybe next Thanksgiving sneak some extra flavonoid-rich spices into the pumpkin pie.

Recommendation:

To keep the peace in your brain, focus on foods rich in flavonoids. The list is long. Just think of herbs, spices, and colorful fruits and vegetables. Beyond the flavonoid-rich foods, Omega-3's, fat soluble vitamins, and the minerals magnesium and zinc are also key nutrients that can help rebalance the body and brain's immune response. Make sure you are regularly taking in fish, seafood, eggs, dairy, a variety of vegetables, herbs and spices, and of course liver!

Eating right (the mental wellness diet way of course), avoiding excess carbohydrates (sugar, junk food, big portions, overeating), exercising (not too much), getting good sleep (7+ hours), and taking control of your stress (see chapter 3) are all required to defend yourself in the modern-day life battle against chronic low grade inflammation. Stay away from environmental toxins like industrial chemicals and plastics. Focus on clean air and water the best you can.

Immune Balancing Nutrients

Vitamin	Function	Food Sources
Vitamin A	Calms activated microglia	liver, sweet potatoes, carrots, cantaloupe, red peppers, mangoes, black-eyed peas, apricots, cheese, eggs, salmon
Vitamin D	Anti-inflammatory	salmon, swordfish, trout, mackerel, herring, mushrooms, cheese, milk
Vitamin E	Calms activated microglia	cheese (pastured/grass-fed), eggs (yolks), pork, oysters, dark chicken, liver

Mineral	Function	Food Sources
Magnesium	Protects against overstimulation of excitatory neurons	pumpkin seeds, almonds, peanuts, sunflower seeds, lima beans, plantains, potatoes, black-eyed peas, apricots, edamame, acorn squash, mussels, shrimp, clams, oysters, summer squash, tomatoes, milk, cheese, blackberries, arugula, dark chocolate (70% or greater)
Zinc	Protects against overstimulation of excitatory neurons	oysters, beef, pumpkin seeds, lobster, lamb, pasilla peppers, edamame, garlic, chickpeas, black-eyed peas, pinto beans, broccoli raab, mushrooms, fish, dark chocolate
Copper	Supports enzyme that breaks down dopamine into norepinephrine;	oysters, sunflower seeds, dark chocolate, almonds, apricots, crab, octopus, lobster, tuna

Selenium	Improves function of dopamine receptors	sunflower seeds, oysters, pumpkin seeds, halibut, swordfish, tuna, lobster, fish roe, fish, pork, chicken, turkey, brazil nuts = 544mcg per ounce

Nutrient	Function	Food Sources
Omega 3's (DHA)	Anti-inflammatory	fish roe, mackerel, salmon, swordfish, oyster, tuna, sardines

Flavonoids	Food Sources
Anthocyanidins	
Cyanidin	raspberries, strawberries, blueberries, blackberries, red cabbage, grapes
Flavon-3-ols	
Catechins	dark chocolate, green tea, white tea, fava beans, raisins, blueberries, cranberries
Proanthocyanidins	apples, berries, red grapes, red wine, chocolate
Flavonols	
Rutin	buckwheat, rooibos tea, figs
Quercetin	red onions, kale, scallions, watercress, apples, berries
Flavones	

Apigenin	parsley, celery, peppermint, thyme
Luteolin	thyme, parsley, peppermint, serrano peppers, celery, chamomile tea, rosemary
Flavonones	
Naringenin	orange, lemon, lime, tangerine, grapefruit
Polyphenols	
Curcumin	turmeric
Resveratrol	red wine, dark chocolate, grapes, peanuts

~ 10 ~

BALANCE

Anxious? Distracted? Uncomfortable?

BALANCED EXCITATION

What do holiday decorations, cologne, and friendly advice all have in common? Less is more. A little goes a long way, and it's easy to overdo it. Decorating for the holidays is a joyous experience. Although the hand-waving, light-up Santa on your front lawn that stays up year-round is just on the other side of tasteful. Finding the right balance is ideal.

I'm sure you've tried to offer advice to a friend whose dealing with a problem (or maybe you have been the victim of this blessing). You listen and give your honest feedback. Yet, somehow, in pointing out the obvious, you've said too much. Suddenly, you see them tense up and you can hear them forcefully exhale. They're on fire and your eyes begin searching for the nearest exit.

From then on, everything you say about the topic is either tight-lipped "mmm hmm" with a nod. Or, if you're feeling brave, you'll go with a compliment sandwich. "Good for you for telling your boss he's a terrible human being and just walking out like that. Seems like it would be good to try and find a new job relatively soon though. I like your shoes?"

When it comes to friendly advice, it's all about balance and knowing your limits. Activity in the brain is no different. As covered in Chapter 8, too much excitation is associated with various mental illness symptomatology.[201,204,219] Excitation is a good thing. But, as we'll learn in this chapter, excitation needs to be balanced out with a healthy amount of inhibition. So, what does it feel like to have too much excitation going on in the brain?

CHANGING THE CHANNEL

There's a lot to the answer of what it feels like when your brain circuits are over-excited. First, it depends on which circuit is being overexcited. Also, the degree of overexcitation matters. Not all of the effects of over-excitation are fully known yet. Research in the field of psychiatry and brain science is now pointed in that direction.[219,220]

Excitation pushes on the gas, over-activating neurons and circuits.[197,219] As a result, there's a lot of noise in the brain. We feel overwhelmed by uneasiness in our body. Our attention is all over the place. And, our minds are racing with a jumble of thoughts and emotions, most of which are negative.

As a side note, the fact that most of our thoughts and feelings when we are overwhelmed are negative actually makes a lot of sense. For us humans to survive, we had to be keenly aware of danger. Without that awareness, one by one early humans would have casually walked up to those wild tigers, with pure intentions of trying to horseplay a little bit, only to be promptly mauled by those adorable furry beasts. Danger sparks fear, and fear drives us to seek safety. Negativity in that sense is a gift. The only problem is that it doesn't feel like much of a gift when we're in it.

Regardless, negativity is the standard operating mode. Why we are often able to spend so much of our time outside of that negativity has to do with the outermost layers of our brains. The outermost layers of the brain, also known as the neocortex – rough translation: the newest part – allow us to perform all of the amazing feats humans are known for. The frontal cortex is one of the major players in this neocortex. I'm not just talking about juggling flaming swords while riding a unicycle. The outermost layer of our brain can preoccupy us with creativity, deep thought, writing, reading, empathizing, art, music, the beauty of nature, and a bunch of other interests that make us human.

By preoccupying our minds with all these interesting things, the outermost layer of our brains is able to cover up all that negativity that swirls around in the deeper, more primal parts of our brains. When we are engaged in some sort of higher level of thought, the more basic emotional circuits in our brain are actively being shushed. That's inhibition at work.

But, there will be times when it happens. Negative thoughts and emotions will breach the barrier and invade our consciousness. It not only feels bad, it can also be kind of surprising. Despite that darker energy always being there (just without our awareness), it's a shock when those intense, often negative, thoughts and emotions rise up from within and splash onto the scene. When they do, it's overwhelming and we just want it to stop. We want to change the channel. So, we reach for things that can hit the brakes. Unfortunately, some of those things can be counterproductive for our mental health. They work in the moment, but at a cost down the road.

What things do we tend to reach for to bring the intensity level down? Mostly, sedating substances like alcohol, marijuana, and other forms of sedating medications (opiates, benzodiazepines like "Xanax"). Carb binges can also do the trick in the moment. In addition, there's a multitude of avoidance behaviors like oversleeping, procrastinating, and indulging in hedonistic pleasures that can help change the channel when needed. These are all common things we instinctively reach for to dial back our reactions to life.[221]

It's not good for us, but often times we can't help it. Again, we are programed for safety. We can easily delude ourselves into thinking that if we close our eyes the monster will go away. Taking something to help gives us that same false sense of security. Some may interpret this as weakness. It's more likely that it's just part of human nature, and our obligation to try to survive. Too much stress all at once can be destabilizing. Stress overstimulates our brain. It also opens the door for excessive excitation.

When our neurons are busy responding to stimulation, there's little resources left over to contribute to the neurons that are working on inhibition. In those moments, we can feel distracted, impulsive, overly emotional, and even experience intrusive anxious or violent thoughts. It's too much, but we don't know what else to do. We've got to dial it back from level 10 somehow.

If only we could find a way to eat, move, think, and live that could prevent these overwhelming upwellings before they got a chance to gain momentum. Well, that way of life would be everything described here in the TMWD. This brings us back to the analogy of the cable box. How many channels does your cable box receive? A thousand? How many channels will your cable box push through at one time? One. Your cable box suppresses 999 channels to let one channel through to your TV. We want our mind to work like that. We want to be able to choose the channel that we are watching. To accomplish that, we need our brain to be able to suppress, block, mute, shush, and tame all the channels that we don't want to watch. One thing at a time. One strong, consistent signal. Minimal background noise.

It's not just intense emotions that can result from relative excess excitation in the brain. Plain old distractibility and brain fog are two other consequences of an imbalance between excitation and inhibition in the brain. Inhibition helps quiet the noise so you can hear the signal.

You want to be able to focus on what you want to focus on. You start out trying to focus on that thing. If you're into this book, then it's likely for you that's not so easy. That noise will pull, tug, beg, persuade, entice, and even bully you into jumping over to another signal – something more interesting or intense. If the noise is loud enough, it will distract you, drown out the signal, and suck you into a hazy vortex where nothing is in focus. The noise should have been muted, but it wasn't. Now you're in free float. The noise that delivers you into the fog stems from all that excessive excitation going on that hasn't been properly muted by inhibition.

As mentioned in Chapter 8, inhibition in the frontal cortex is important for giving us pause. Inhibition helps us stop and think before we react impulsively.[184,219] That millisecond of uninterrupted focus allows us to actually do something productive. We want that ability to pause. In the frontal cortex, inhibition allows us focus on the task at hand, for longer than 10 seconds. Beyond preventing distractions, the frontal cortex also helps us cope with stress. It allows us to take a second to breathe before we drown in an uncomfortable emotional soup.[222] It helps us momentarily resist that internal fear that tries to convince us that it's all going to end very badly unless we react right now.[222] A level 10 threat requires a level 10 reaction, right? The frontal cortex offers us poise and purpose. The tool it uses to give us these gifts is inhibition.

As you may have gathered by now, it's tough out there in modern-day life. Numerous environmental factors in modern life can activate our nervous[223-224] and immune systems.[225-226] Yet, our human brain has the machinery to handle a fair degree of stress and distractions. That's how inhibition became such a big part of the human brain circuitry. Thanks to inhibition, we can do and not do at the same time. For those of us experiencing distractibility, anxiety, depressed moods, and all other kinds of mental illness symptoms, it's liberating when we can find a way to do what we need to without being dragged down by all the stuff going on in our brains that we don't want or need to be happening.

As with everything, balance is key. We have established that when it comes to chemical and electrical activity in the brain, inhibition is equally as important and necessary as excitation. The balance of both allows for balance in our lives.[227]

FAST AND FURIOUS

Electrical activity in the brain needs to find a balance between excitation and inhibition for us to feel and function well.[219] Think about how we drive. Our cars have two pedals: gas and brake. If your car only had a gas pedal (excitation), and no brake (inhibition), that would be problematic. With just a gas pedal to work with, you wouldn't make it very far before you crashed into something. The brake is necessary. It helps us slow down so we can avoid danger, stop when we need to, and steer ourselves in the right direction.

Inhibition is about tapping on the brakes as you bend into the turns. Gently tapping on the brakes allows you to continue moving forward, but in a controlled way. We tap on the brakes so that we can steer in the direction that we want to go. We need inhibition (the brake) as a counterbalance at certain times and places, as well as to certain degrees. Just as you wouldn't slam on your brake, come to a dead stop, then make a turn, inhibition is not about a full stop. It's more like a light tap on the brake to ease you into the turn.

However, we can't forget about excitation (the gas pedal). The gas pedal takes us places. Without it, the car would be useless. Excitation mediates all our brain functions. It helps us learn, memorize, think, adapt, and process our emotions.[228]Without excitation we'd be useless blobs. Both excitation and inhibition are important. The take home point here is that unopposed excitation is a common problem that leads to a lot of mental and emotional unrest. The balance between the two is essential.

It's kind of like my aunt who drives with two feet (there's definitely going to be a family meeting right after this book is published). Intermittently she'll tap on the gas with her left foot, but she's always working the brake with her right – just in case. This makes for a complicated relationship between my Aunt and her mechanic, but she's okay with it. It helps her feel like she's in control. This may not be the best way to maintain the life of your car, but it's an effective strategy for your brain to try and maintain stability in this crazed modern-day life.

We need to seek the healthy balance point between excitation and inhibition. A healthy balance between the gas and brake in our brain helps us feel active, engaged, and in control. Always tapping on the brake in this or that brain circuit provides us with that same sense of control. It ensures that we never overdo it with thoughts, perceptions, and feelings.

HOUSE OF CARDS

In real life, inhibition doesn't shut us down completely. Just a little pressure in the opposite direction of excitation does us a world of good. Inhibition is gentle, but constant pressure, like your favorite pair of skinny jeans.

Our human brain developed this very elaborate network of checks and balances over time. It's a delicate system of inhibitory neurons intersecting with excitatory ones. The inhibitory neurons, interlaced with the excitatory neurons, are poised to tap on the brake when our excitatory neurons start to pick up speed or activity. When the brain is functioning optimally, it's a house of cards. Response and absence of response in perfect balance.

The risk we face in modern-day life – from all the inflammation-promoting foods, toxins, and stress – is the overstimulation of our brain circuits. Our brains possess a massive potential for excitatory reaction, and these environmental stimuli turn that potential into reality.[229-230] If we're smart about things, inhibition will be there as the traffic officer in a busy intersection. It lets the excitatory signals it deems most important at that moment come on through, but blocks, mutes, and filters out the rest. If inhibition can adequately put excitation into check, it will help us feel and act more in control.[231]

This inhibitory counterbalance to excitation in the brain is vital to our mental stability and emotional regulation.[231] Again, the balance of both allows for balance in our lives.[226] The key is to support our inhibitory mechanisms with diet and lifestyle. At the same time, we need to try our best to avoid the toxic environmental factors that trigger excessive excitation.

For most neurons, excitation is mediated by common electrolytes – sodium, potassium, calcium, and chloride. The body does a great job at conserving these electrolytes, so for most of us, there's no need to worry about getting enough of these electrolytes in the diet. Even in the Western pattern diet, it's not hard to consume enough. And, not to worry, these electrolytes are also plentiful in TMWD.

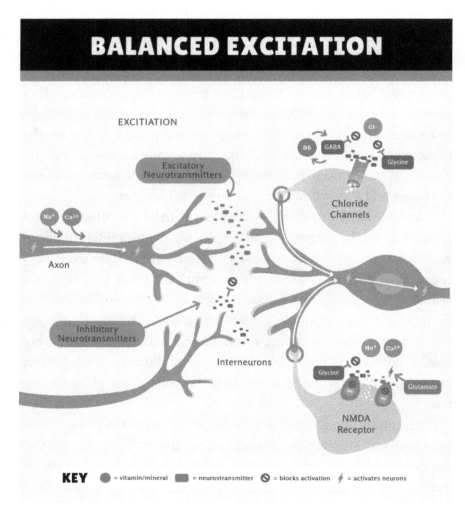

BALANCED EXCITATION

KEY ● = vitamin/mineral ▇ = neurostransmitter ⊘ = blocks activation ⚡ = activates neurons

• *Sodium and Calcium are needed for normal electrical activity in the brain.*

• *Vitamin B6, the amino acids Taurine and Glycine, as well as the minerals Magnesium and Zinc act as buffers against excitation.*

What are the nutrients that support inhibition? First, it's important to note that GABA (gamma aminobutyric acid) is the primary inhibitory neurotransmitter. It's massively important for inhibition. As you can imagine from the description of excitation and inhibition above, GABA is being utilized all the time. With so much use, the supply of GABA can become depleted. Vitamin B6 plays a critical role recycling GABA, so it can be there to help out with inhibition when the brain needs.[190, 232]

Similarly, the amino acid glycine can step in and act as an inhibitory neurotransmitter.[233] The same is true for the amino acid taurine.[234] Both of these amino acids make it harder for excitatory receptors to fire those excitatory neurons. They don't fully block excitation. It's more like they gently pull back on the excitatory throttle.

Then there are a couple of key minerals that provide a similar counterbalance against excitation. Magnesium squeezes inside the excitatory (known as NMDA) receptors, thus blocking the ability of sodium and/or calcium from entering and activating the receptor.[235-236] Zinc binds to the outer aspect of the NMDA receptor, which deactivates the receptor function and thus diminishes the excitatory activity in the brain.[237] These key nutrients do not bring excitation to a full stop. They just tap on the brake, so the brain doesn't go overboard.

Outside of nutrition, meditation and mindfulness can make a difference. Remember how riding a bike gets easier the more you practice. The same is true with meditation and mindfulness. With practice you can definitely get better at bringing your attention back to what you want. That goal of mindfulness practice is not to immediately deliver you to a place of serenity and peace every time. Meditation and mindfulness practices are hard work. It's often an uncomfortable struggle, just as it is with learning how to ride a bike. Through practice, we can train our brain to get better at inhibiting thoughts and feelings that inevitably bubble up. This enhances our ability to focus and regulate our emotions in the future.

Recommendation:

Let's start with Vitamin B6. The allium family of vegetables are full of B6. Think of ways to jazz up your cooking with garlic, onions, scallions, chives, leeks, and shallots. That's a twofer. The alliums make your meals all the more savory. And, they'll hand you with a steady supply of GABA boosting Vitamin B6.

Next up is glycine. Homemade bone broth is a great source. That takes planning and time, however. Another great option is collagen peptide powder. Collagen peptide powder is a clean, easy, versatile source of glycine. You can add this powder to soups and smoothies, or just put a couple scoops into hot water with a tea bag and drink it down quick and easy.

For the chill-out benefits of taurine, magnesium, and zinc, focus on incorporating more seafood, beans, nut and seeds.

On the lifestyle side of things, try to make sure you take in a healthy dose of self-forgiveness every day. Life is tough, and none of us are perfect. Failure and struggle are essential parts of life. With time and persistence, you will be able to get where you want to go.

The trick is to push yourself to be better at responding, rather than reacting. The first step is to gain awareness of distractions, anxious thoughts, and dark emotions when they bubble up – you got to name it to tame it. The second step is accepting the fact that distractions and emotions will undoubtedly bubble up. It's just part of being human.

The third step is a hard one. When negative emotional states do emerge, try to avoid the guilt, shame, and all other negative self-assessments that accompany these negative emotional states. Realizing you're distractible and emotional can make us feel bad. Try to stop those thoughts in their tracks because thinking that way feeds the beast and keeps you trapped. This step is so much easier said than done, so don't be afraid to ask for some help – a friend, family, therapist, pastor, pet, even writing it out helps. Again, it's all part of being human. For the fourth step, decide to act in accordance with your principles.

Decide where you want to go in life and then figure out which channel you need to be tuned into to get there. If your brain's cable box is going to suppress 999 channels to just let one through, which channel do you want to watch?

Brain Balancing
Nutrients

Vitamin	Function	Food Sources
Vitamin B6	Recycles inhibitory neurotransmitter GABA	pasilla peppers, red peppers, chives, shallots, onions, parsley, garlic, leeks, prunes, apricots, bananas, eggs, cheese, tuna, salmon
Glycine	Acts as inhibitory neurotransmitter	bone broth, collage peptide powder
Taurine	Acts as inhibitory neurotransmitter	dark chicken/turkey meat, beef, pork, lamb, salami, tuna, mussels, clams, scallops, squid, oysters

Magnesium	Protects against overstimulation of excitatory neurons	pumpkin seeds, almonds, peanuts, sunflower seeds, lima beans, plantains, potatoes, black-eyed peas, apricots, edamame, acorn squash, mussels, shrimp, clams, oysters, summer squash, tomatoes, milk, cheese, blackberries, arugula, dark chocolate (70% or greater)
Zinc	Protects against overstimulation of excitatory neurons	oysters, beef, pumpkin seeds, lobster, lamb, pasilla peppers, edamame, garlic, chickpeas, black-eyed peas, pinto beans, broccoli raab, mushrooms, fish, dark chocolate

~ 11 ~

CONCLUSION

You Got This...

KEEP MOVING FORWARD

Forward momentum is an essential feature of mental wellness. In life, it is so easy to get stuck. It's especially easy to get stuck in negativity. Remember that negativity was originally designed to help protect us from danger. The self-protective instinct used to work just fine. It helped get us to where we are today. Yet, stuck means that whatever the problem or negativity in your life, you are now drowning in it. This is why moving forward is so important. We can't be attending to negativity, disappointment, frustration, offensive people, or even self-doubt when we are moving forward. Instead, forward momentum is about investing the energy and resources that we do have into the health of our body and mind, as well as our purpose.

In modern-day life, the game has changed. Nowadays, we're unfortunately pushed too far in some ways (constant social pressure, toxic food and environment, addictive bright light phones, the rent's too damn high), and sadly not enough in other ways (sedentary lives, ease of isolation, always using a calculator, absence of play in adulthood). Fear and negativity flood our lives - they rev us up and hold us back at the same time. Modern-day life is hard and too easy at the same time. So, when life throws us challenges, it feels really hard because so much else in our lives is hard. But, it's also hard because we're metaphorically, and literally, out of shape.

TMWD is not about making your life easier. If your life was easy, that would be unfortunate. Without struggle, you would never meet the person you are truly meant to become. TMWD is about being mindfully selective about which struggles we invite into our lives. Should we put energy into anxiety over things that truly don't matter? Or, should we put that energy into trying to move forward?

Does 24/7 connectivity, social media-induced competition, or the feeling that we need to try to change ourselves into something we think others would like better add to your mental well-being? It doesn't.

These useless challenges presented by modern-day life make you less functional. They simply sap your energy, make you feel bad about yourself, and prevent you from discovering what truly makes you tick. We can't grow and move forward in life if fear, negativity, and scattered thinking keep us stuck at the starting line. Modern-day life is sneaky. It knows how to pull you away from your purpose, towards its own. Should you go for that hike with friends, or another time because there's a new TV show just out that you can binge watch?

In what other ways does modern-day life attempt to pull you towards its own purpose? It lies to you and tells you there's an easier way. It tells you that you don't need to feel uncomfortable. It knows someone who invented a solution for that. Modern-day life can get you to avoid challenges that are actually good for you. It makes you take a pass on challenges that build resilience. It's actually these challenges that can help you meet your true self. They often seem hard, grueling, uncomfortable, but these big challenges will also make you question what really matters to you.

If modern-day life was able to convince you to do duck face in your selfies, it likely also convinced you to lean into the comfort.

Too much comfort makes us weak. It also makes us strangers to ourselves. We have to be careful. Start to think about some of your discomforts in life as challenges. These challenges may be opportunities. Once overcome, you may feel better than you did before these challenges entered your life.

Think about the challenge of finding the time and motivation to start exercising? Once you find a way to tolerate the initial discomfort, your experience of working out is transformed from grueling agony and self-doubt into newfound strength and confidence. Once you reach that point, you'll feel worse on days you don't get a chance to exercise. The same is true for your meditation practice and all other forms of self-discipline.

Think of good food, good sleep, connection, nature, self-acceptance, self-forgiveness, and meaning & purpose as essential nutrients that you must consume daily. These essential daily nutrients won't bring success right away. But they'll strengthen you and help you put in the effort to continue moving forward. These daily nutrients will build more efficient and durable brain circuits, give your brain the energy and resources it needs to respond, and help it find the balance between excitation and inhibition.

We need these daily nutrients because life is tough. We need every advantage we can possibly give to ourselves. It's never easy to start eating better. It's equally difficult to stop, take a second to breathe, and simply let go of intense negative emotions. Facing the pain, discomfort, or even boredom that often accompanies starting your meditation practice can be, well, painful.

Learning to tolerate sitting with ourselves at critically important moments for sure helps in the long run. But it's also uncomfortable. Remember the hazards of exceptionalism? The danger is that trying to start out with an expectation that you will be awesome at eating well, exercising, meditating, and being a social rock star all at once. This expectation may feel good to fantasize about, but as you've likely experienced before, harboring those unrealistic expectations tends to cut you down at the knees before you even get a chance to begin.

Stealing time away from our busy schedules to make time to sunbathe leaves us with a nice base tan but doing so might open up the door of our mind to anxiety about all the things we didn't get done while loafing under the sun. This is the mindset we need to change.

First, sunbathing is never a waste of time. Second, worrying about what you should have been busy doing or accomplishing is the real waste of time. Best to strike a balance. When it's time to work, feel that pressure and stress and let it push you. When work is finished, then it's time to switch gears. However, you can stop, exhale, and find a way to let go of all that anxiety and stress still tugging on you. The same mantra from childhood still applies. Get your stuff done so then you can go out and play.

For me, writing this book was challenging. Finding the time to write, then re-write, then edit some more felt impossible most days. Squeezing in time for this book meant sacrifice. In worrying if I'd ever finish, or even if anyone would find it valuable, I sacrificed my peace of mind. In constantly struggling to focus late at night – frequently my only time to dedicate to the project – I sacrificed my sleep, which meant that my typically pleasant personality was often sacrificed the following day. In working for hours on end at my desk, permanently hunched over like Gollum, I sacrificed my body (and not in the heroic sense). The worst sacrifice, however, was on the part of my family. During this time, they did not get 100% of me, which they deserved. For that sacrifice I'll be forever grateful, and maybe a little guilty.

Why did I break all my own rule? Well, I'm human, and humans do this sort of thing. And, I'm living in modern-day life too. I guess it just felt like something I needed to do. There were some altruistic reasons, along with some related to pride, vanity, and maybe even greed. Let's just focus on the altruistic reasons, mm-kay?

Getting my thoughts down on paper was really important for me. I strongly believe in what I wrote in this book. I feel the principles behind TMWD are sound and really important for everyone to know about. In discovering how the brain and body can contribute to mental wellness (or illness), I felt I had to put this together. In addition, I have seen the guidance from this book work in my own life, as well as in the lives of my patients. This book, fortunately or unfortunately, has been my meaning and purpose. Now that it's complete and out there, I have come home to my family, returned to my healthy habits, and ran with open arms back to my love of sunbathing.

Setting out to write this invited into my life many of those toxic stressors of modern-day life – self-consciousness and unnecessary competition, late nights, skipped meals, and the occasional (frequent) carb binge to help cope with all that stress. When that happened, I had to find a way to reset. I had to figure out a way to dial it back and get back to basics.

Even before I could reset by eating better, getting outside, prioritizing sleep, spending more quality time with friends and family, I had to gain an awareness of what was happening. It was so easy to get sucked into all the pressure and stress. It's common. Take a little over here, give a little over here. Despite my best efforts at denial, I was sliding further and further away from my typical healthy habits. It wasn't easy trying to climb my way back into good daily habits and eating patterns. There were weeks and months in between where I just had to step away and take a break. That was almost as painful as the consequences of slacking on my self-care.

Yet, in the end, all this back and forth struggle was instructive. I eventually found a degree of balance between work and self-care, but at a cost. It's easy to write down a list of things that you should do to be healthy. It's much harder to live it. There was a kind of poetic justice to the mental, emotional, and physical struggles I experienced during the year or so I spent writing.

In dedicating myself to write a book about the ancestral dietary and lifestyle principles that can lead us to mental wellness, I, at times, neglected most all of these same principles. With such a big undertaking, there was pressure to finish. Plus, I had a number of other responsibilities to keep up with. Any delay was painful. Those breaks offered me time to let my thoughts marinade, which actually made for a better final product. But having to wait, or feeling held back by competing priorities, opened the door for fear, doubt, worry, and the urge to sacrifice my mental wellness in so many ways – just to get it done. Those forces definitely tipped me off balance. Ironically, during this time, it was mentally challenging to decide to prioritize my physical and emotional health.

Below are some final thoughts on the lessons gained from this experience. My hope in sharing is that it helps you find a way to have the courage and confidence to continue to search for the balance as you set out to incorporate the TMWD guidance into your life. Here's a summary of some of the lessons I've learned along the way that helped me get back up after I stumbled.

First, as you proceed, prioritize the goals that add to, rather than subtract from, your energy and self-esteem. TMWD is chock full of activities that are good for you... movement, sleep, getting outdoors, spending time with friends. Start there. Lucky for me, my children were more persuasive than storylines I had in my head about this project (needing to spend every spare second on getting it done, or else...). In a way that only children can do, they forced me to unglue myself from the pressure and stress when I needed. They helped me to do the simple things like take breaks, eat snacks, and soak in the beauty around me.

Second, spend some time thinking about your life's purpose. Identify what makes you feel good after you do it, versus what makes you feel good while you're doing it. There needs to be a balance of instant versus delayed gratification. It's okay to have fun – it's actually necessary for mental wellness. But for a deeper sense of wellness, you have to be pushing towards something greater. That solo journey up the mountain hurts and heals at the same time. So, determine what you want in life, and what's important to you. Name it, either out loud or written down. Then do what you can to make it happen – for yourself versus for others in your life. Starting small works. In time, you'll develop the momentum you need to tackle the bigger stuff.

Finding a balance between instant and delayed gratification is tricky. Discovering meaning and purpose is the first, best way to get started. Fun will find a way into your life if your mind is calm and quiet enough to receive it. Spend your days working towards your purpose, and that calm and quiet are likely to be there when you wake up the next day.

Third, be aware of the fact that our modern life is chaotic and borderline unfair. The toxicity of modern-day life is always lurking in the background, ready to swallow us up when we're looking the other way. Practicing self-forgiveness is the key to being able to continue moving forward. Finding ways to move on and let go is the hallmark of mental wellness. When you're getting it done on a daily basis, other's negativity can't touch you. Reacting to negativity with negativity halts that forward progress we need to stay mentally well. Moving on starts with self-forgiveness. Tomorrow will always come. There will always be another chance to do better. Just keep going the best you can.

Please consider the guidance here as a template rather than an instruction manual. Figure out what will work for you. Just remember that we humans have needs – food that fuels our brain, clean air and water, movement, social networks, and fun. We can't be well without attending to these needs. This book provides just a sample of some of the ways to meet these needs. You will know how to fill in the blanks, because you know which direction you want to go. Now, go!

~ 12 ~

MODERN-DAY OPTIONS

Ready Already?

WHAT TO EAT:
Thanks for hanging in there! There has been a lot of science and philosophy to get through just to get to the 'what do I eat' part of the book. Hope the journey was worth it. Or, maybe you just scrolled ahead to this page right here. If you jumped ahead and missed all the science, then that just means you must be ready to get started!

Either way, here is TMWD in two short lists.

Eat the foods on the What's In list. Avoid, or really limit, the foods on the What's Out list.

WHAT'S IN:
The list includes foods that are healthy, but also ones that tend to have a higher amount of key nutrients that support brain health.

- Organ Meats: (difficult to stomach, but so important) liver, kidneys, heart are the common ones Shellfish: oysters, mussels, clams, scallops, shrimp, squid

- Animal Meat: (organic, grass-fed, pasture-raised) chicken, lamb, beef, pork, and other game meat Eggs: (organic and/ or pasture-raised preferred)
- Fish: salmon, mackerel, tuna, swordfish, trout, herring fish roe
- Bone Broth: (from bones versus just meat)
- Healthy Fats: (for cooking) Extra-virgin Olive Oil , Coconut Oil, Ghee, (for salads) Avocado Oil
- Starchy Vegetables: (organic if possible) broccoli, cauliflower, acorn squash, butternut squash, peas
- Non-starchy Vegetables: (organic if possible) lettuces, spinach, cabbage, dandelion greens, swiss chard, kale, carrots, red/orange/yellow peppers, asparagus, parsley, spirulina, chives, pasilla peppers, leeks, garlic, onion, Brussels sprouts, green beans, beets, zucchini, summer squash, broccoli rabe
- Mushrooms: White, Cremini, Shiitake, Portabella
- Fruits: (organic if possible) avocados, apricots, mangoes, cantaloupe, plantains, oranges, blackberries, raspberries, blueberries, grapes, dates, figs, bananas, kiwi
- Nuts & Seeds: almonds, walnuts, sunflower seeds, pistachios, pumpkin seeds, pine nuts, flaxseeds, tahini (sesame seeds)
- Seaweed: Nori, Duse, Wakame, Kelp, Kombu, Arame
- Fermented Foods: Kimchi, Sauerkraut, Kefir
- Herbs and spices: all herbs and spices are included
- Chocolate: dark chocolate, greater than 70% preferred
- Beans: black-eyed peas, edamame, kidney beans, pinto beans, chickpeas
- Rice: white, brown, jasmine
- Oats: (steel cut, instant)
- Dairy: (depends on individual tolerance, preferred organic, raw if more nutrient dense) milk, cheese, yogurt

WHAT'S OUT:

Many of these foods are often consumed when we are busy, on the run, out with friends, or somehow forgot to eat and ended up starving. These foods will call to you during those times. Best to be prepared and plan ahead with the What's In food list and provided recipes.

- Animal Meat: (factory farmed)
- Grains: Wheat
- Soy: anything other than edamame
- Sugar: sweets, added in processed foods/drinks
- Processed Foods: chips, crackers, cookies, pastas, frozen dinners, white bread, and even energy bars. If it has a label or comes in a plastic package, it is likely not good for you or your brain
- Alcohol: beer, wine, spirits
- Soda: all
- Juices: all
- Vegetable Oils: (canola, soy, sunflower, grapeseed)

~ 13 ~

RECIPES

What to Eat When Life's Eating You

Here's some recipes to get you started. These recipes were intentionally curated not to annoy or frustrate you. Feel like you can't cook? Not to worry, most all of these recipes will be easy enough to prepare without any yelling, cursing, or dejection. The focus is on ease of preparation, simplicity, and highlighting nutrients our brains need the most.

Juices & Smoothies

TRIPLE BERRY SMOOTHIE
Makes 2 servings
  Ingredients
  2 medium bananas, sliced and frozen
  1 cup unsweetened cow's milk, almond or macadamia nut milk
  1 cup frozen strawberries
  1 cup frozen blueberries
  1 cup frozen raspberries
  Directions

1. Add bananas into the blender. Blend until the bananas become crumbly.
2. Add milk. Blend until smooth and creamy, scraping down the sides of the blender as needed.
3. Add strawberries, blueberries and raspberries. Blend until smooth, again, scraping down the sides of the blender as needed.
4. Pour into two cups and enjoy.

RED ROOIBOS SMOOTHIE
Makes 1 serving
  Ingredients
  1 frozen banana
  3 frozen strawberries
  8 oz steeped red rooibos tea (chilled)
  Directions

  1. Steep the tea for 5-7 minutes, and make sure to chill the tea for about 15 minutes
  2. Blend all ingredients together until smooth. 3. Pour into a glass and enjoy!

Note: steep the tea for 5-7 minutes, and make sure to chill the tea for about 15 minutes before using it in the smoothie

BMOC (BANANA, MANGO, ORANGE, COCONUT WATER)
Makes 2 servings
  Ingredients
  2 peeled oranges
  1/2 cup frozen mango chunks
  1 banana
  1/2 - 1 cup coconut water
  Directions

1. Add all ingredients into a high-powered blender and blitz until blended. 2. Add coconut water to desired consistency.

Breakfast

MEAT & VEGGIE FRITTATA

Makes 4 servings

Ingredients

1 lb ground beef or pork sausage (casings removed)

1 tbsp coconut oil or EVOO

1.cup of vegetables: kale, broccoli, cauliflower, onions, peppers, mushrooms, etc.

8 whole eggs, whisked

Onion or garlic powder

Sea salt and pepper

Chopped fresh basil, tomato slices, or shredded cheese for garnish (optional)

Directions

1. Preheat your oven to 350 degrees. Heat the oil over medium heat in 10" cast iron skillet
2. Crumble the meat in the pan and cook, breaking it up as it cooks so it browns evenly. *Add the crushed red pepper now if you wish for extra spice.
3. Once your meat is toasty brown, remove from skillet and set aside
4. Add vegetables to the pan and stir frequently
5. In a large bowl, whisk your eggs well with onion/garlic powder, salt & pepper
6. Pour egg mixture over sausage mixture slowly to cover.
7. Top the egg/sausage mixture with sliced tomatoes, basil, or cheese.

8. Bake in the preheated oven 20 minutes, or until the eggs are solid and edges begin to turn golden brown.
9. Let it sit to cool and set a bit, and then either serve or wrap and refrigerate/freeze for later use.

KBO (KALE, BACON, ONIONS WITH EGGS)
Makes 2 servings
Ingredients
2. eggs
3-4 strips bacon

1. tbsp coconut oil or EVOO
2. handfuls of chopped or baby kale

1/2 medium onion, diced
Directions

1. Heat sauté pan or skillet over medium heat
2. Add bacon to pan, turning once, cook until brown
3. Remove bacon with tongs, cut into 1" pieces on cutting board, and set aside
4. Soak up some of grease with paper towels, and remove once hot with tongs (optional)
5. Add diced onion to pan with remaining grease, cook until translucent
6. Add kale on top of onions, and turn over and stir until kale wilts down
7. Add bacon back into pan
8. Make space in middle of skillet with tongs
9. Crack eggs into middle of pan, turn down heat to low, cook until whites fully solid

ROOIBOS OATMEAL
Makes 1 serving

Ingredients

1-2 organic instant oatmeal packets

1 rooibos tea bag

1/2 Tbsp virgin/unrefined coconut oil

1 scoop collagen peptide powder

Salt to taste

Directions

1. Heat water in tea kettle or pot
2. Steep Rooibos tea bag in 4oz of steaming hot water for 5 minutes
3. Combine hot water to oatmeal packets, oil, collagen powder & salt, and stir

Salads

THREE BEAN SALAD

Makes 6 servings

Ingredients

For the salad & dressing:

1 (15-ounce) can cannellini beans, rinsed and drained

1 (15-ounce) can kidney beans, rinsed and drained

1.(15-ounce) can garbanzo beans, rinsed and drained

1/2 red onion, finely chopped (about 3/4 cup)

2.celery stalks, finely chopped (about 1 cup)

1 cup loosely packed, fresh, finely chopped flat-leaf parsley

1 tsp fresh finely chopped rosemary

1/3 cup apple cider vinegar

1/4 cup coconut sugar

3 Tbsp extra virgin olive oil 1-1/2 tsp salt

1/4 teaspoon black pepper

Directions

1. Place chopped red onion in a small bowl of water for 10minutes
2. Combine three kinds of beans, soaked onions, celery, parsley, and rosemary in a large bowl and toss together
3. In a separate bowl, whisk together the dressing ingredients - apple cider vinegar, EVOO, coconut sugar, salt & pepper 4. Add the dressing to the bean mixture and toss
4. Refrigerate for a couple hours to let dressing soak into the beans and vegetables
5. Serve chilled

MAGNESIUM BOMB
Makes 1 serving
Ingredients
For the salad:
2 handfuls of mixed greens or arugula
1 (15-ounce) can black beans, rinsed and drained
1 handful slivered almonds or 1 handful pumpkin seeds
1 small avocado, sliced
1 Tbsp EVOO
1 tsp lemon juice or half lemon fresh squeezed
Salt to taste
Black pepper to taste
For the salmon:
1 salmon filet, rinsed, patted dry
1 tbsp EVOO
1/2 tsp Italian seasonings or herbs de Provence
Salt & black pepper to taste
Directions

1. Preheat oven to 350 degrees
2. Place salmon on aluminum foil on baking sheet, cover with EVOO and seasonings

3. Bake salmon for 20-25 minutes
4. Pull out salmon and let cool
5. Combine greens, black beans, nuts in large bowl
6. Toss with EVOO, lemon juice, salt & pepper
7. Top with avocado and salmon

BUCKWHEAT TABBOULEH
Makes 4 servings
Ingredients
1 cup buckwheat groats
1 cup cherry tomatoes, chopped into quarters 1 mango, diced
1.cucumber, diced
2 large handfuls fresh parsley, chopped fine
1 large handful fresh mint, chopped fine
1 lemon (juiced and grated)
1/4 cup red onion or spring onion, chopped fine 2 garlic cloves, minced
2 Tbsp EVOO
Salt to taste
Black pepper to taste
Directions

1. Bring 2 cups of water to a boil on medium heat.
2. Add in the buckwheat and cook for 10 minutes with the lid off, until most of the water is absorbed
3. Turn the heat down to low with the lid on for a few more minutes until all the water is gone and the buckwheat is soft.
4. Fluff the buckwheat up with a fork and set to cool while you prepare everything else.
5. Add the remaining ingredients to a large bowl
6. Transfer the buckwheat to the bowl and toss well until all ingredients are combined

Salad Dressing

ESSENTIAL FOUR

1 lemon, fresh squeezed

  2 Tbsp olive oil

  Salt to taste

  Black pepper to taste

  Directions

  1. Add all four ingredients to green salads, toss with tongs or salad spoons
  Apple Cider Vinegar Dressing
  1/4 cup apple cider vinegar
  1/2 cup olive oil
  2. teaspoons Dijon mustard

1 tablespoon garlic, minced

  1. teaspoon sea salt + more if needed

1/2 teaspoon freshly ground black pepper to taste + more if needed

Directions

  1. Add all ingredients into a blender and blend until combined or add to a mason jar and shake to combine.
  2. Taste and add more salt and pepper to taste if needed.

LEMON TAHINI DRESSING

1/4 cup tahini

  2. tablespoons fresh lemon juice

  1 tablespoon apple cider vinegar 2 cloves garlic, minced

  1 tablespoon pure maple syrup Salt to taste

  Pepper to taste

  1/4 cup water to thin

Directions

1. Pour all ingredients into a small bowl or jar.
2. Whisk together until smooth.
3. If the tahini flavor is too strong for your taste, add a bit more apple cider vinegar and syrup to taste.

Snacks

TART CHERRY GUMMIES
Makes 4 Servings
Ingredients
1-1/2 cup organic tart cherry juice (not from concentrate)
1/4 cup raw honey
1/2 cup beef gelatin powder
Directions

1. Pour 1 cup of cherry juice into unheated pan
2. Add beef gelatin powder and stir immediately
3. Mix together until no more powder is visible
4. Turn on stove to medium heat
5. Add remaining 1/2 cup cherry juice and 1/2 cup honey
6. Sir frequently while mixture warms
7. Heat until mixture starts to bubble, then take off heat
8. Pour into silicon molds right away
9. Let cool on counter for 30 minutes
10. Place in refrigerator for 2 hours before eating

BAKED PLANTAINS
Makes 6 servings
Ingredients
3 ripe plantains (dark yellow with black spots)
3 Tbsp EVOO or melted coconut oil
1 tsp salt

Directions

1. Preheat the oven to 425 degrees F
2. Line a large baking sheet with parchment paper
3. Cut the ends off each plantain and score the peels from end to end, making sure not to cut through the plantains
4. Pull the peels off and discard
5. Slice the plantains on an angle to make longer pieces, 1/4- to 1/3-inch thick
6. Pile the plantain slices on baking sheet and drizzle with oil
7. Toss to coat all the plantain strips on both sides
8. Lay them out in a single layer
9. Sprinkle generously with salt
10. Bake the plantains for 10 minutes
11. Flip and bake another 10 minutes
12. Serve warm or at room temperature

ROASTED CHICKPEAS
Makes 2 servings
Ingredients

1. can chickpeas 2. tsp salt

2 Tbsp olive oil
Then, choose a topping option:

FOR SPICED MAPLE FLAVOR:
1 tsp paprika
1/4 tsp cayenne pepper
1 tsp chili powder
1/4 cup maple syrup

FOR TURMERIC AND LIME FLAVOR:
1/2 tsp ginger

2 tsp turmeric
Juice from 1 lime

FOR CINNAMON SUGAR FLAVOR:
1 tsp ground cinnamon
1/4 cup coconut sugar

FOR RANCH FLAVOR:
1/2 tsp dried thyme
1 tsp minced onion
1 tsp dried dill
1/2 tsp garlic powder
1/2 tsp pepper
Directions

1. Toss chickpeas with salt and olive oil, coating evenly.
2. Spread chickpeas on a baking sheet and roast at 450 for 20 minutes.
3. Toss with desired flavor ingredients and enjoy.

Dinners

LEBANESE LEMON CHICKEN
Makes 6-8 servings
Ingredients
3 lemons
2.tbsp olive oil
1/2 tsp ground turmeric
1-1/2 tsp flaky sea salt
3.lb. boneless, skinless chicken thighs (about 12 thighs)
2 large shallots or 1 large onion
2 sprigs fresh rosemary
2 sprigs fresh thyme
Directions

1. Juice one of the lemons until you have 2 tablespoons of lemon juice. Put the juice in a large bowl and add the 2 tablespoons of olive oil along with the turmeric, sea salt, and a generous amount of freshly ground black pepper.
2. Add the chicken thighs to the bowl and toss to coat. Let the chicken marinate briefly at room temperature while you prepare the other ingredients.
3. Trim the ends off the other two lemons and slice them into 1/4-inch thick rounds. Remove any visible seeds. Halve, peel, and slice the shallots.
4. Heat two large cast iron skillets over medium-high heat (or use one skillet and cook the chicken in two batches). Add enough olive oil to coat the bottom with a thin layer of oil.
5. Divide the chicken pieces between the two pans with the smooth side of the chicken (where the skin was) facing down, making sure to leave a little room between the pieces so they can brown. Cook for about 5 minutes, until nicely browned on the bottom, and then flip and cook for 8-10 minutes on the second side, until just cooked through, lowering the heat slightly if necessary. Use tongs or a slotted spatula to transfer the chicken pieces to a plate.
6. Add the lemons, shallots, and herb sprigs to the pans. Let cook undisturbed for 3-4 minutes, until the lemons are browned on the bottom. Pour 1/2 cup water into each pan and stir, scraping the browned bits from the bottom. Reduce the heat to medium, add the chicken back to the pans, and cook for 4-5 minutes so the flavors can meld. Serve the chicken, shallots, and pan juices hot over rice or cauliflower rice.

KITCHARI
Makes 6 servings
Ingredients
2 Tbsp ghee or unrefined virgin coconut oil

1 Tbsp mustard seeds (yellow or brown)
1/2 Tbsp cumin seeds
1-2 pinch crushed red chili flakes
1.cup dried split yellow mung beans, rinsed
1 cup brown or white basmati rice, rinsed
2 large carrots, cut into large chunks
1-1/2 tsp ground turmeric
1.tsp ground coriander
8 cups water
2.cups finely chopped kale, spinach, beet greens or Swiss chard
1-1/2 tsp sea salt + more to taste
Directions

1. Heat oil in a large stockpot
2. Add mustard seeds, cumin seeds, and chili flakes and gently sauté over medium heat until the seeds begin to pop
3. Add the mung beans, rice, carrots, turmeric and coriander. Stir together a bit so the spices evenly coat the rice and beans
4. Then add the water and bring the stew to a boil
5. Once boiling, cover and simmer on low for about 45 minutes
6. Feel free to simmer longer, for a thicker consistency
7. Once the rice and beans are cooked, add the chopped greens and salt
8. Stir until just mixed well
9. Turn off heat, cover, and let stand for about 5 minutes, until greens are tender.
10. Taste for salt

STUFFED PASILLAS
Makes 4 servings
Ingredients
3.chorizo sausage links or 1/2 lb ground beef

2 fresh pasilla peppers, seeded and cut in half lengthwise

4 small-medium mushrooms, diced

1 Tbsp diced onion

1 tsp minced garlic

1/2 cup shredded cheddar or Monterey jack cheese

Directions

1. Preheat oven to 375 degrees
2. Heat pan over medium heat
3. Brown meat (take casing off of chorizo prior to cooking)
4. Once meat is browned, add mushrooms, onion & garlic
5. Cook for 3 minutes
6. Line peppers up in shallow baking dish or pie pan
7. Fill each pepper half with meat mixture
8. Top with shredded cheese
9. Bake 20-25 min

SPAGHETTI SQUASH WITH MEATBALLS

Makes 4-6 Servings

Ingredients

For the spaghetti squash:

1 large spaghetti squash

1 tbsp EVOO

Salt to taste

Pepper to taste

For the sauce & meatballs:

1.lb ground beef

1 large egg

1/4 cup coconut flour

1/4 tsp dried basil

1 tsp salt

1/4 tsp garlic powder

2.tsp Italian seasonings

3/4 tsp black pepper

1/4 tsp paprika
1/4 tsp red pepper flakes (optional)
1/2 cup shredded Parmesan cheese (optional)
2 tbsp EVOO
24 oz glass jar of pasta sauce
Directions

1. Preheat oven to 400 degrees
2. Cut spaghetti squash in half, lengthwise from stem to stem
3. Scoop out seeds and loose strands
4. Rub spaghetti squash with EVOO, salt, & pepper
5. Place spaghetti squash cut sides up, bake 1 to 11/4 hour, until soft to fork poke
6. Combine ground beef, coconut flour, egg, and dry seasonings in large bowl
7. Form mixture into 1-1/2 inch meatballs
8. Heat 2 tbsp EVOO in pan over medium heat
9. Cook meatballs about 6 minutes, turning often until brown on all sides
10. Pour sauce from jar into saucepan and head on medium
11. Add meatballs to saucepan and simmer, covered on low-medium heat
12. Pull out squash and allow to cool a few minutes
13. When cool enough to handle, scrape out the flesh with a fork
14. Serve bed of shredded spaghetti squash topped with sauce and meatballs

Perfect Meats

PERFECT STEAK
Makes 1-2 Servings
  Ingredients
  10 oz New York Strip steak

2 tbsp EVOO
Salt to taste
Pepper to taste
Directions

1. Preheat oven to 350 degrees
2. Place steaks on counter at room temperature for 20-30 minutes
3. Rub steak with dash of salt and generous amount of pepper
4. Heat EVOO in case iron skillet on medium-high heat
5. Wait until skillet is hot, wet hands and flick water into pan, if it sizzles, it's ready
6. Sear steak 3 minutes each side
7. Remove skillet from stove and place in 350-degree oven
8. Bake for 5 minutes
9. Remove and cover with aluminum foil for 5-10 minutes
10. Plate medium-rare steak and serve

*Clean cast iron skillet when still warm. Use with just warm water and stainless-steel scrubbing pad. Do not use dish or other soap. Once clean dry immediately with towel. Rub small amount of EVOO over inside of skillet and store in dry place.

CHICKEN THIGHS
Makes 4 Servings
Ingredients
6 skin-on, bone-in chicken thighs
1 tbsp EVOO
Salt to taste
Pepper to taste
Directions

1. Preheat oven to 475 degrees

2. Rinse chicken thighs and pat dry with paper towels
3. Heat EVOO in case iron skillet on medium-high heat
4. Wait until skillet is hot, wet hands and flick water into pan, if it sizzles, it's read
5. Place chicken thighs, skin side down in preheated skillet
6. Cook 2 minutes
7. Reduce heat to medium, continue cooking skin side down for 12 minutes
8. Rotate chicken thighs in pan to cook evenly
9. Remove skillet from stove and place in 475-degree oven
10. Cook another 13 minutes
11. Flip chicken thighs, and cook another 5 minutes
12. Remove from oven, cover with aluminum foil, and let rest for 5 minutes, plate and serve

*Clean cast iron skillet when still warm. Use with just warm water and stainless-steel scrubbing pad. Do not use dish or other soap. Once clean dry immediately with towel. Rub small amount of EVOO over inside of skillet and store in dry place.

PORK TENDERLOIN
Makes 4 Servings
Ingredients
1-1/2 to 2 lbs pork tenderloin
4 tbsp EVOO
Salt to taste
Pepper to taste
Italian seasonings
Directions

1. Preheat oven to 400 degrees
2. Unpack pork tenderloin, if present, remove top layer of fat with sharp knife

3. Poke holes in pork tenderloin
4. Rub with EVOO, salt, pepper, and Italian seasonings
5. Heat EVOO in case iron skillet on medium-high heat
6. Wait until skillet is hot, wet hands and flick water into pan, if it sizzles, it's read
7. Sear pork tenderloin on all sides, 1-2 minutes each side, total 6 minutes
8. Remove skillet from stove and place in 400-degreeoven
9. Cook another 15-20 minutes
10. Measure internal temperature with meat thermometer, make sure reading is 145-155 degrees F
11. Remove from oven, cover with aluminum foil, and let rest for 5 minutes
12. Plate and serve

*Clean cast iron skillet when still warm. Use with just warm water and stainless-steel scrubbing pad. Do not use dish or other soap. Once clean dry immediately with towel. Rub small amount of EVOO over inside of skillet and store in dry place.

GARLIC BUTTER LOBSTER TAILS
Makes 4 servings
Ingredients
1 lb. shell-on lobster tails (about 4 tails)
1/2 stick salted butter, melted (4 tbsp)
4 cloves garlic, minced
1.tbsp chopped parsley
1/2 lemon, sliced
1/2 lemon, squeezed for juice
Directions

1. Preheat the broiler on your oven. (Thaw the lobster tails if they're frozen.)

2. Using a pair of kitchen scissors, cut through the top part of the lobster shell lengthwise, towards the tail
3. Peel back lobster tail meat from inside of shell
4. Pull lobster shell outward and apart to expose the lobster meat
5. Arrange the lobsters on a baking sheet or tray, meat side up
6. Melt the butter in a glass dish or small saucepan on the low-medium heat on the stove
7. Once butter is fully liquid, add the garlic, parsley and lemon juice, and stir to mix well
8. Drizzle and spread the garlic butter mixture on the raw lobster, but save some for dipping
9. Broil the lobster tails in the oven about 5-8 minutes (top rack, but at lease 2" below flame)
10. Broil until the lobster meat turns opaque and fully cooked through
11. Serve immediately with the remaining garlic butter and lemon slice

Soups

RHODE ISLAND CLAM CHOWDER
Makes 4 servings
Ingredients
2.cups canned clams
1/4 lb or 4 ounces thick cut bacon (3 slices), diced
1 tbsp butter
1 whole yellow onion, diced
3 stalks celery, diced
3.cups chicken broth
1 cup water
4.sprigs thyme
2 bay leaves
1 lb red potatoes, diced into small cubes

Salt to taste
Black pepper to taste
Chopped parsley to taste
Directions

1. Rinse and strain canned clams and set aside
2. Heat large, heavy Dutch oven to medium-low and add butter, heat until partially melted
3. Add the bacon and cook, stirring and flipping occasionally, about 5 minutes
4. Once bacon is browned, use tongs to remove bacon from fat and set aside
5. Add onions and celery to the remaining fat, and cook, stirring frequently, until they are soft but not brown, about 10 minutes
6. Stir in potatoes and wine, and continue cooking until the wine has evaporated and the potatoes have just started to soften, approximately 5 minutes
7. Add 3 cups of chicken broth and 1 cup of water
8. Add the thyme and the bay leaf
9. Partly cover the pot, and simmer gently until potatoes are tender, approximately 10 to 15 minutes
10. Meanwhile, chop the bacon into small 1/2-inch pieces
11. When the potatoes are tender, stir in the chopped clams and bacon 12. Add black pepper to taste
12. Let the chowder come just to a simmer and remove from heat
13. Fish out the thyme and bay leaf, and discard
14. The chowder should be allowed to sit for a while to cure
15. Reheat it before serving, then garnish with chopped parsley

CAULIFLOWER BROCCOLI SOUP
Makes 6 servings

Ingredients
1 head broccoli, cut into individual florets
1 head cauliflower, cut into individual florets
1 leek, split down the middle, outer layer removed, sliced
2 carrots, chopped
3 stalks of celery, chopped
1 large onion, chopped
5 cloves of garlic
Garlic salt to taste
Salt to taste
Pepper to taste
2.tbsp EVOO
1/2 stick butter
3.cups chicken broth
2 cups water
1-2 scoops of collagen powder per serving
Directions

1. Heat EVOO in large, heavy Dutch oven over medium
2. Add carrots, celery, onion, and leeks and cook until soft and onions are translucent
3. Add garlic, and cook for 1-2 minutes until golden brown
4. Add broth and water
5. Add cauliflower and broccoli
6. Partly cover the pot, and simmer gently until cauliflower/broccoli are tender, approximately 10 to 15 minutes
7. Remove from stove and place Dutch oven on towel on the counter
8. Add 1/2 stick of butter
9. Use immersion/hand blender, and puree broth, vegetables, and butter until consistent
10. Ladle into bowls and serve

11. Optional – add 1-2 scoops of collagen peptide powder into bowls of soup

ROASTED BUTTERNUT SQUASH SOUP

Makes 8 servings

Ingredients

1 large butternut squash

2 carrots, chopped

3 stalks of celery, chopped

1 large onion, chopped

5.cloves of garlic

6 sage leaves

6.sprigs of thyme

1 sprig of rosemary

Salt to taste

Pepper to taste

2 tbsp EVOO

1/4 stick butter

3 cups chicken broth

1 cup water

Directions

1. Preheat the oven to 350 degrees
2. Peel, pit and chop the butternut squash into 1-inch squares
3. Add butternut squash to a large baking pan
4. Add the carrots, celery and onions to the pan
5. Add whole garlic cloves
6. Add the herbs (stems are removed), salt and pepper
7. Add olive oil and toss to coat
8. Roast for 1 to 1-1/4 hour until veggies are soft and tender, especially the carrots
9. Transfer cooked vegetables to large, heavy Dutch oven with 3 cups of chicken broth and 1 cup of water

10. Add 1/4 stick of butter
11. Use immersion/hand blender, and puree broth and vegetables until consistent
12. Turn stove to medium until soup begins to simmer, then reduce to low for 1 minutes
13. If the consistency of the soup is too thick, just thin it out with some water until you reach your desired consistency.
14. Ladle into bowls and serve

SLOW COOKER BONE BROTH
Makes 4 Servings
Ingredients
2 carrots, chopped
2 celery stalks. chopped
1 onion, chopped
8-10 garlic cloves, crushed
3-4 pounds beef bones
2 bay leaves
Salt to taste
Pepper to taste
2 tablespoons apple cider vinegar
Enough water to fill slow cooker
Directions

1. Plug in 6 quart slow cooker on counter away from other items.
2. Place chopped veggies and garlic in the bottom of slow cooker
3. Place bones on top of veggies
4. Add apple cider vinegar and enough water to fill slow cooker almost to rim
5. Turn slow cooker to low

6. Let cook on low for 8-10 hours, don't open lid while it slow cooks
7. Open lid, fish out and throw out the bones and veggies
8. Grab the ceramic bowl insert and strain broth into another dish/bowl
9. Throw out the remaining veggies, bay leaves, solid bits
10. Enjoy broth right away
11. Save remainder in fridge for a few days, or in freezer for a few months

Sides

BAKED SWEET POTATOES

Makes 6 servings

Ingredients

3 sweet potatoes, washed and scrubbed 2 tbsp EVOO

Salt to taste

Directions

1. Preheat the oven to 400 degrees
2. Cut the sweet potatoes in half, lengthwise
3. Place the potatoes on a baking sheet or glass baking dish
4. Drizzle oil on the sweet potatoes, then rub the oil on the flesh and skins of each potato
5. Sprinkle each potato with salt
6. Place sweet potatoes flesh-side down on the baking sheet or glass baking dish
7. Bake the sweet potatoes, uncovered, for 30-35 minutes, until the skins begin to look shriveled and soft
8. Remove the potatoes from the oven, the baked sweet potatoes should be slightly brown and caramelized on the top of the flesh and soft throughout the potato

9. Enjoy the sweet potatoes warm, or place them in an airtight container in the fridge to enjoy later in the week

BROCCOLI KALE SLAW
Makes 8 servings
Ingredients
For the slaw:
1.12-ounce package broccoli slaw
2 cups finely chopped kale
1/2 cup dried cranberries
1/2 cup slivered almonds
For the dressing:
1/3 cup white wine vinegar
1/4 cup EVOO
2.tbsp coconut sugar
1 tsp Dijon mustard
1/2 tsp celery seed Salt to taste
Directions

1. Place all vinaigrette ingredients in a mason jar with a tight-fitting lid and shake well
2. Combine the broccoli slaw ingredients in a large serving bowl
3. Toss with vinaigrette and serve

ROASTED CAULIFLOWER
Makes 6-8 servings
Ingredients
1.head of cauliflower, chopped into florets
3 cloves of garlic, crushed
2.tbsp EVOO
1 tbsp turmeric powder
1 tsp cumin powder
1 tsp paprika

1 tsp coriander
Salt to taste
Directions

1. Preheat the oven to 350 degrees
2. In a bowl combine the olive oil, spices and garlic
3. Add cauliflower florets to bowl
4. Toss cauliflower with oil and spices so florets are evenly coated
5. Spread the cauliflower across 1-2 baking sheets lined with parchment paper
6. Bake the cauliflower for 15-20 minutes, until the cauliflower starts to brown
7. Remove from the oven and serve

PICNIC POTATO SALAD
Makes 4 servings
Ingredients
1-1/2 pounds fingerling potatoes, cut into large pieces
1/4 cup EVOO
Fresh thyme, chopped
Salt to taste
Black pepper to taste
1.tbsp red wine vinegar
2 tsp coarse-grained mustard
1 tsp coconut sugar
4 slices bacon, browned and cut into pieces
1 small bunch green onions, chopped
Directions

1. Place cut potatoes in a large pot and cover with water
2. Turn stove to high, boil potatoes until fork tender

3. In a medium sized mason jar add the oil, thyme, salt, pepper, vinegar, mustard and sugar.
4. Shake to combine
5. Drain cooked potatoes
6. Dump potatoes into a medium bowl
7. Pour mixture over hot potatoes
8. Add bacon and green onions
9. Toss to coat and serve

Desserts

DARK CHOCOLATE & ALMOND BUTTER

70% or higher dark chocolate bar 2 tbsp almond butter
   Salt to taste
   Directions

1. Spoon almond butter into ramekin or bowl, scoop out with pieces of dark chocolate bark
2. sprinkle salt on almond butter if desired

FROZEN BERRIES CEREAL

10 ounce bag of frozen organic mixed berries (or other fruit)
   1 cup milk (dairy, almond, coconut, macadamia nut milk)
   Directions

1. Pour milk over berries
2. Let sit on counter until frozen berries begin to soften
3. Eat like cereal

FIG & DATE BALLS

Makes 24 Balls
   Ingredients
   1.cup Medjool dates pitted
   1 cup dried figs

2.2-1/2 cups raw cashews
1 cup unsweetened shredded coconut
1 tbsp chia seeds
1.tbsp hemp seeds
2.teaspoons pure vanilla extract
1 pinch sea salt
Directions

1. Add all ingredients for the fig and date balls to a food processor
2. Blend until a sticky dough forms
3. Scoop out with spatula into a large glass baking dish
4. Roll dough into desired-sized balls and enjoy!
5. Balls should be stored in a sealable bag or container in the refrigerator or freezer.

~ 14 ~

REFERENCES

1. Aarts,E.,Ederveen,T.,Naaijen,J.,Zwiers,M.,Boekhorst,J.,Timmerman,H., Smeekens, S., Netea, M., Buitelaar, J., Franke, B., Hijum, S., Vasquez, A. (2017). Gut microbiome in ADHD and its relation to neural reward anticipation PloS one 12(9).

2. Cenit,M.,Sanz,Y.,Codoñer-Franch,P.(2017).Influence of gut microbiota on neuropsychiatric disorders World Journal of Gastroenterology 23(30), 5486 -5498.

3. Cenit,M.,Nuevo,I.,Codoñer-Franch,P.,Dinan,T.,Sanz,Y.(2017).Gut microbiota and attention deficit hyperactivity disorder: new perspectives for a challenging condition European child & adolescent psychiatry 26(9), 1081 -1092.

4. Kelly,J.,Kennedy,P.,Cryan,J.,Dinan,T.,Clarke,G.,Hyland,N.(2015).Breaking Down the Barriers: The Gut Microbiome, Intestinal Permeability and Stress-related Psychiatric Disorders Frontiers in Cellular Neuroscience 9(2), 215.

5. Mitchell,R.,Goldstein,B.(2014).InflammationinChildrenandAdolescentsWith Neuropsychiatric Disorders: A Systematic Review Journal of the American Academy of Child and Adolescent Psychiatry 53(3), 274 - 296.

6. Raison,C.,Capuron,L.,Miller,A.(2006).Cytokinessingthe-blues:inflammation and the pathogenesis of depression Trends in Immunology 27(1), 24 - 31.

7. Berk,M.,Williams,L.,Jacka,F.,O'Neil,A.,Pasco,J.,Moy-lan,S.,Allen,N.,Stuart, A., Hayley, A., Byrne, M., Maes, M. (2013). So depression is an inflammatory disease, but where does the inflammation come from? BMC medicine 11(1), 200.

8. Vogelzangs,N.,Beekman,A.,Jonge,P.,Penninx,B.(2013).Anxi-etydisorders and inflammation in a large adult cohort Translational psychiatry 3(4), e249 - e249.

9. Pitsavos,C.,Panagiotakos,D.,Papageorgiou,C.,Tset-sekou,E.,Soldatos,C., Stefanadis, C. (2006). Anxiety in relation to inflammation and coagulation markers, among healthy adults: The ATTICA Study Atherosclerosis 185(2), 320 - 326.

10. Salzer, H. (1966). Relative Hypoglycemia as a Cause of Neuropsychiatric Illness Journal of the National Medical Association 58(1), 12.

11. Timonen,M.,Laakso,M.,Jokelainen,J.,Rajala,U.,Meyer-Ro-chow,V., Keinänen-Kiukaanniemi, S. (2004). Insulin resistance and depression: cross sectional study BMJ 330(7481), 17 - 18.

12. Tomlinson, D., Wilkinson, H., Wilkinson, P. (2009). Diet and Mental Health in Children Child and Adolescent Mental Health 14(3), 148 - 155.

13. Rao, T., Asha, M., Ramesh, B., Rao, K. (2008). Understanding nutrition, depression and mental illnesses. Indian journal of psychiatry 50(2), 77 - 82.

14. Dhar, A., Barton, D. (2016). Depression and the Link with Cardiovascular Disease Frontiers in Psychiatry 7(1), 130.

15. Hayes, J., Miles, J., Walters, K., King, M., Osborn, D. (2015). A systematic review and meta-analysis of premature mor-

tality in bipolar affective disorder Acta Psychiatrica Scandinavica 131(6), 417 - 425.

16. Watanabe, N., Furukawa, T., Chen, J., Kinoshita, Y., Nakano, Y., Ogawa, S., Funayama, T., Ietsugu, T., Noda, Y. (2010). Change in quality of life and their predictors in the long-term follow-up after group cognitive behavioral therapy for social anxiety disorder: a prospective cohort study BMC Psychiatry 10(1), 81.

17. WILLIAMS, P. (2007). Nutritional composition of red meat Nutrition & Dietetics 64(s4 The Role of), S113 - S119.

18. U.S.Department of Agriculture (USDA), Agricultural Research Service.FoodData Central:Foundation Foods. Version Current:March2019. Internet:www.fdc.nal.usda.gov

19. Finkelstein, J. (1990). Methionine metabolism in mammals The Journal of Nutritional Biochemistry 1(5), 228 - 237.

20. Meléndez-Hevia, E., Paz-Lugo, P., Cornish-Bowden, A., Cárdenas, M. (2009). A weak link in metabolism: the metabolic capacity for glycine biosynthesis does not satisfy the need for collagen synthesis Journal of Biosciences 34(6), 853 - 872.

21. Venugopal, V., Gopakumar, K. (2017). Shellfish: Nutritive Value, Health Benefits, and Consumer Safety Comprehensive Reviews in Food Science and Food Safety 16(6), 1219 - 1242.

22. Milton, K. (1999). A hypothesis to explain the role of meat-eating in human evolution Evolutionary Anthropology: Issues, News, and Reviews 8(1), 11 - 21.

23. Pereira, P., Vicente, A. (2013). Meat nutritional composition and nutritive role in the human diet Meat Science 93(3), 586 – 592.

24. Micronutrients, I. (2001). Dietary Reference Intakes for Vitamin A, Vitamin K, Arsenic, Boron, Chromium, Copper,

Iodine, Iron, Manganese, Molybdenum, Nickel, Silicon, Vanadium, and Zinc.

25. Obeid, R., Heil, S., Verhoeven, M., Heuvel, E., Groot, L., Eussen, S. (2019). Vitamin B12 Intake From Animal Foods, Biomarkers, and Health Aspects. Frontiers in nutrition 6(), 93.

26. Daley, C., Abbott, A., Doyle, P., Nader, G., Larson, S. (2010). A review of fatty acid profiles and antioxidant content in grass-fed and grain-fed beef NutritionJournal 9(1), 1 - 12.

27. Johnston, B., Zeraatkar, D., Han, M., Vernooij, R., Valli, C., Dib, R., Marshall, C., Stover, P., Fairweather-Taitt, S., Wójcik, G., Bhatia, F., Souza, R., Brotons, C., Meerpohl, J., Patel, C., Djulbegovic, B., Alonso-Coello, P., Bala, M., Guyatt, G. (2019). Unprocessed Red Meat and Processed Meat Consumption: Dietary Guideline Recommendations From the Nutritional Recommendations (NutriRECS) Consortium. Annals of internal medicine.

28. Tamang, J., Watanabe, K., Holzapfel, W. (2016). Review: Diversity of Microorganisms in Global Fermented Foods and Beverages. Frontiers in microbiology 7(350), 377. https://dx.doi.org/10.3389/fmicb.2016.00377

29. Tamang, J., Shin, D., Jung, S., Chae, S. (2016). Functional Properties of Microorganisms in Fermented Foods Frontiers in microbiology 7(e40945), 6358.

30. Course, M., Wang, X. (2016). Transporting mitochondria in neurons F1000Research 5(1735), 1735 - 10.

31. Wallace, C., Milev, R. (2017). The effects of probiotics on depressive symptoms in humans: a systematic review. Annals of General Psychiatry 16(1), 14 - 10.

32. Tillisch, K., Labus, J., Kilpatrick, L., Jiang, Z., Stains, J., Ebrat, B., Guyonnet, D., Legrain-Raspaud, S., Trotin, B., Naliboff, B., Mayer, E. (2013). Consumption of fermented milk product with probiotic modulates brain activity. Gastroenterology 144(7), 1394 - 401- 1401.e1-4.

33. Wacker, M., Holick, M. (2013). Sunlight and Vitamin D Dermato-Endocrinology 5(1), 51 - 108.

34. Baeke, F., Takiishi, T., Korf, H., Gysemans, C., Mathieu, C. (2010). Vitamin D: modulator of the immune system Current Opinion in Pharmacology 10(4), 482 - 496.

35. Aranow, C. (2011). Vitamin D and the Immune System Journal of Investigative Medicine 59(6), 881 - 886.

36. Fisher, S., Rahimzadeh, M., Brierley, C., Gration, B., Doree, C., Kimber, C., Cajide, A., Lamikanra, A., Roberts, D. (2019). The role of vitamin D in increasing circulating T regulatory cell numbers and modulating T regulatory cell phenotypes in patients with inflammatory disease or in healthy volunteers: A systematic review. PloS one 14(9).

37. Cui, X., Gooch, H., Petty, A., McGrath, J., Eyles, D. (2017). Vitamin D and the brain: Genomic and non-genomic actions. Molecular and Cellular Endocrinology 453(), 131 - 143.

38. Kiraly, S., Kiraly, M., Hawe, R., Makhani, N. (2006). Vitamin D as a Neuroactive Substance: Review The Scientific World Journal 6(), 125 - 139.

39. Patrick, R., Ames, B. (2014). Vitamin D hormone regulates serotonin synthesis. Part 1: relevance for autism. FASEB journal : official publication of the Federation of American Societies for Experimental Biology 28(6), 2398 - 2413.

40. Kaneko, I., Sabir, M., Dussik, C., Whitfield, G., Karrys, A., Hsieh, J., Haussler, M., Meyer, M., Pike, J., Jurutka, P. (2015). 1,25-Dihydroxyvitamin D regulates expression of the tryptophan hydroxylase 2 and leptin genes: implication for behavioral influences of vitamin D. FASEB journal : official publication of the Federation of American Societies for Experimental Biology 29(9), 4023 - 4035.

41. Holick, M. (2002). Vitamin D: the underappreciated D-lightful hormone that is important for skeletal and cellular

health Current Opinion in Endocrinology, Diabetes and Obesity 9(1), 87.

42. Fleury, N., Geldenhuys, S., Gorman, S. (2016). Sun Exposure and Its Effects on Human Health: Mechanisms through Which Sun Exposure Could Reduce the Risk of Developing Obesity and Cardiometabolic Dysfunction International journal of environmental research and public health 13(10), 999.

43. Hasegawa, Y., Arita, M. (2014). Circadian clocks optimally adapt to sunlight for reliable synchronization. Journal of the Royal Society, Interface 11(92), 20131018.

44. Remi, J. (2015). Humans Entrain to Sunlight - Impact of Social Jet Lag on Disease and Implications for Critical Illness. Current pharmaceutical design 21(24), 3431 - 3437.

45. Morita, T., Tokura, H. (1996). Effects of Lights of Different Color Temperature on the Nocturnal Changes in Core Temperature and Melatonin in Humans Applied Human Science 15(5), 243 - 246.

46. Duffy, J., Czeisler, C. (2009). Effect of Light on Human Circadian Physiology Sleep Medicine Clinics 4(2), 165 - 177.

47. Leproult, R., Colecchia, E., L'Hermite-Balériaux, M., Cauter, E. (2001). Transition from Dim to Bright Light in the Morning Induces an Immediate Elevation of Cortisol Levels The Journal of Clinical Endocrinology & Metabolism 86(1), 151 - 157.

48. Stewart, K., Kelemen, M., Ewart, C. (1994). Relationships Between Self-Efficacy and Mood Before and After Exercise Training Journal of Cardiopulmonary Rehabilitation and Prevention 14(1), 35.

49. Annesi, J., Unruh, J. (2008). Relations of Exercise, Self-Appraisal, Mood Changes and Weight Loss in Obese Women: Testing Propositions Based on Baker and Brownell's (2000)

Model The American Journal of the Medical Sciences 335(3), 198 - 204.

50. Ide, K., Secher, N. (2000). Cerebral blood flow and metabolism during exercise Progress in Neurobiology 61(4), 397 - 414.

51. Secher, N., Seifert, T., Lieshout, J. (2008). Cerebral blood flow and metabolism during exercise: implications for fatigue Journal of Applied Physiology 104(1), 306 - 314.

52. Vecchio, L., Meng, Y., Xhima, K., Lipsman, N., Hamani, C., Aubert, I. (2018). The Neuroprotective Effects of Exercise: Maintaining a Healthy Brain Throughout Aging Brain Plasticity 4(1), 17 - 52.

53. Huang, E., Reichardt, L. (2003). Neurotrophins: Roles in Neuronal Development and Function1 dx.doi.org 24(1), 677 - 736.

54. Binder, H. (2004). Brain-derived Neurotrophic Factor Growth factors (Chur, Switzerland) 22(3), 123 - 131.

55. Heyman, E., Gamelin, F., Goekint, M., Piscitelli, F., Roelands, B., Leclair, E., Marzo, V., Meeusen, R. (2012). Intense exercise increases circulating endocannabinoid and BDNF levels in humans—Possible implications for reward and depression Psychoneuroendocrinology 37(6), 844 - 851.

56. Griffin, É., Mullally, S., Foley, C., Warmington, S., O'Mara, S., Kelly, Á. (2011). Aerobic exercise improves hippocampal function and increases BDNF in the serum of young adult males Physiology & Behavior 104(5), 934 - 941.

57. Hashimoto, K., Shimizu, E., Iyo, M. (2004). Critical role of brain-derived neurotrophic factor in mood disorders Brain Research Reviews 45(2), 104 - 114.

58. Duclot, F., Kabbaj, M. (2015). Epigenetic mechanisms underlying the role of brain-derived neurotrophic factor in depression and response to antidepressants. Journal of Experimental Biology 218(1), 21 - 31.

59. Zong, H., Ren, J., Young, L., Pypaert, M., Mu, J., Birnbaum, M., Shulman, G. (2002). AMP kinase is required for mitochondrial biogenesis in skeletal muscle in response to chronic energy deprivation Proceedings of the National Academy of Sciences 99(25), 15983 - 15987.

60. Dreyer, H., Fujita, S., Cadenas, J., Chinkes, D., Volpi, E., Rasmussen, B. (2006). Resistance exercise increases AMPK activity and reduces 4E-BP1 phosphorylation and protein synthesis in human skeletal muscle The Journal of Physiology 576(2), 613 - 624.

61. Tarnopolsky, M. (2009). Mitochondrial DNA shifting in older adults following resistance exercise trainingThis paper article is one of a selection of papers published in this Special Issue, entitled 14th International Biochemistry ofExercise Conference – Muscles as Molecular and Metabolic Machines, and has undergone the Journal's usual peer review process. Applied Physiology, Nutrition, and Metabolism 34(3), 348 - 354.

62. Kim, J., Wei, Y., Sowers, J. (2008). Role of Mitochondrial Dysfunction in Insulin Resistance Circulation Research 102(4), 401 – 414.

63. Fariss, M., Chan, C., Patel, M., Houten, B., Orrenius, S. (2005). ROLE of MITOCHONDRIA in TOXIC OXIDATIVE STRESS Molecular Interventions 5(2), 94 - 111.

64. Mailloux, R. (2018). Mitochondrial Antioxidants and the Maintenance of Cellular Hydrogen Peroxide Levels Oxidative Medicine and Cellular Longevity 2018(), 1 - 10. https://dx.doi.org/10.1155/2018/7857251

65. Tschopp, J. (2011). Mitochondria: Sovereign of inflammation? European Journal of Immunology 41(5), 1196 - 1202.

66. López-Armada, M., Riveiro-Naveira, R., Vaamonde-García, C., Valcárcel-Ares, M.(2013). Mitochondrial dysfunction

and the inflammatory response Mitochondrion 13(2), 106 - 118.

67. Wang, D., Kinoshita, C., Kinoshita, Y., Morrison, R. (2014). p53 and mitochondrial function in neurons Biochimica et Biophysica Acta (BBA) – Molecular Basis of Disease 1842(8), 1186 - 1197.

68. Course, M., Wang, X. (2016). Transporting mitochondria in neurons F1000Research 5(1735), 1735 - 10.

69. Voss, M., Weng, T., Narayana-Kumanan, K., Cole, R., Wharff, C., Reist, L., DuBose, L., Sigurdsson, G., Mills, J., Long, J., Magnotta, V., Pierce, G. (2019). Acute Exercise Effects Predict Training Change in Cognition and Connectivity. Medicine and science in sports and exercise Publish Ahead of Print(), 1.

70. Stathopoulou, G., Powers, M., Berry, A., Smits, J., Otto, M. (2006). Exercise Interventions for Mental Health: A Quantitative and Qualitative Review Clinical Psychology: Science and Practice 13(2), 179 – 193.

71. Vidoni, E., Johnson, D., Morris, J., Sciver, A., Greer, C., Billinger, S., Donnelly, J., Burns, J. (2015). Dose-Response of Aerobic Exercise on Cognition: A Community-Based, Pilot Randomized Controlled Trial PloS one 10(7), e0131647.

72. Herring, M., O'Connor, P., Dishman, R. (2010). The Effect of Exercise Training on Anxiety Symptoms Among Patients: A Systematic Review Archives of internal medicine 170(4), 321 - 331.

73. Hankin, B. L., & Abela, J. R. Z. (2005). Development of psychopathology: A vulnerability-stress perspective. Thousand Oaks, Calif: Sage Publications.

74. Liguori, I., Russo, G., Curcio, F., Bulli, G., Aran, L., Della-Morte, D., Gargiulo, G., Testa, G., Cacciatore, F., Bonaduce, D., Abete, P. (2018). Oxidative stress, aging, and diseases Clinical Interventions in Aging 13(), 757 - 772.

75. Wang, L., Muxin, G., Nishida, H., Shirakawa, C., Sato, S., Konishi, T. (2007). Psychological Stress-Induced Oxidative Stress as a Model of Sub-Healthy Condition and the Effect of TCM Evidence-based complementary and alternative medicine : eCAM 4(2), 195 – 202.

76. Cui, H., Kong, Y., Zhang, H. (2011). Oxidative Stress, Mitochondrial Dysfunction, and Aging Journal of Signal Transduction 2012(3), 1 - 13.

77. Ask, T., Lugo, R., Sütterlin, S. (2018). The Neuro-Immuno-Senescence Integrative Model (NISIM) on the Negative Association Between Parasympathetic Activity and Cellular Senescence. Frontiers in Neuroscience 12(), 726.

78. Dantzer, R., O'Connor, J., Freund, G., Johnson, R., Kelley, K. (2008). From inflammation to sickness and depression: when the immune system subjugates the brain Nature reviews. Neuroscience 9(1), 46 – 56.

79. Dantzer, R. (2009). Cytokine, Sickness Behavior, and Depression Immunology and Allergy Clinics of North America 29(2), 247 - 264.

80. Miller, A., Haroon, E., Raison, C., Felger, J. (2013). CYTOKINE TARGETS IN THE BRAIN: IMPACT ON NEUROTRANSMITTERS AND NEUROCIRCUITS Depression and anxiety 30(4), 297 - 306.

81. Karshikoff, B., Sundelin, T., Lasselin, J. (2017). Role of Inflammation in Human Fatigue: Relevance of Multidimensional Assessments and Potential Neuronal Mechanisms Frontiers in Immunology 8(), 21.

82. Fernández-Sánchez, A., Madrigal-Santillán, E., Bautista, M., Esquivel-Soto, J., Morales-González, Á., Esquivel-Chirino, C., Durante-Montiel, I., Sánchez-Rivera, G., Valadez-Vega, C., Morales-González, J. (2011). Inflammation, Oxidative Stress, and Obesity International Journal of Molecular Sciences 12(5), 3117-3132.

83. Cherbuin, N., Anstey, K., Baune, B. (2017). Oxidative stress, inflammation and mild cognitive impairment European Psychiatry 41(), S742.

84. Jackson M. Evaluating the Role of Hans Selye in the Modern History of Stress. In: Cantor D, Ramsden E, editors. Stress, Shock, and Adaptation in the Twentieth Century. Rochester (NY): University of Rochester Press; 2014 Feb. Chapter 1.

85. Boonstra, R. (2013). Reality as the leading cause of stress: rethinking the impact of chronic stress in nature Functional Ecology 27(1), 11 - 23.

86. McEwen, J. (2010). What's in a name? Integrating homeostasis, allostasis and stress Hormones and behavior 57(2), 105 - 111.

87. Chetty, S., Friedman, A., Taravosh-Lahn, K., Kirby, E., Mirescu, C., Guo, F., Krupik, D., Nicholas, A., Geraghty, A., Krishnamurthy, A., Tsai, M., Covarrubias, D., Wong, A., Francis, D., Sapolsky, R., Palmer, T., Pleasure, D., Kaufer, D. (2014). Stress and glucocorticoids promote oligodendrogenesis in the adult hippocampus Molecular Psychiatry 19(12), 1275-1283.

88. Schneiderman, N., Ironson, G., Siegel, S. (2004). Stress and Health: Psychological, Behavioral, and Biological Determinants dx.doi.org 1(1), 607 - 628.

89. Lindahl, J., Fisher, N., Cooper, D., Rosen, R., Britton, W. (2017). The varieties of contemplative experience: A mixed-methods study of meditation-related challenges in Western Buddhists. PloS one 12(5), e0176239.

90. Lewis, R. (2014, June 2). How Different Cultures Understand Time.

91. Vaish, A., Grossmann, T., Woodward, A. (2008). Not all emotions are created equal: The negativity bias in social-emotional development. Psychological Bulletin 134(3), 383.

92. Folkman, S., Lazarus, R., Dunkel-Schetter, C., DeLongis, A., Gruen, R. (1986). Dynamics of a stressful encounter: cognitive appraisal, coping, and encounter outcomes. Journal of personality and social psychology 50(5), 992 - 1003.

93. Creswell, J., Taren, A., Lindsay, E., Greco, C., Gianaros, P., Fairgrieve, A., Marsland, A., Brown, K., Way, B., Rosen, R., Ferris, J. (2016). Alterations in Resting- State Functional Connectivity Link Mindfulness Meditation With Reduced Interleukin- 6: A Randomized Controlled Trial Biological Psychiatry 80(1), 53-61.

94. Mineo, L. (2018, November 26). Over nearly 80 years, Harvard study has been showing how to live a healthy and happy life. Retrieved from https:// news.harvard.edu/ gazette/story/2017/04/over-nearly-80-years-harvard-study- has- been-showing-how-to-live-a-healthy-and-happy-life/

95. Aiello, L., anthropology, R., 1993Neocortex Size, Group Size, and the Evolution of Language | Current Anthropology: Vol 34, No 2 journals.uchicago.edu

96. Goyal, M., Singh, S., Sibinga, E., Gould, N., Rowland-Seymour, A., Sharma, R., Berger, Z., Sleicher, D., Maron, D., Shihab, H., Ranasinghe, P., Linn, S., Saha, S., Bass, E., Haythornthwaite, J. (2014). Meditation Programs for Psychological Stress and Well-being: A Systematic Review and Meta-analysis JAMA Internal Medicine 174(3), 357-368.

97. Teo, A., Choi, H., Valenstein, M. (2013). Social Relationships and Depression: Ten-Year Follow-Up from a Nationally Representative Study PloS one 8(4), e62396.

98. Santini, Z., Koyanagi, A., Tyrovolas, S., Haro, J. (2015). The association of relationship quality and social networks with depression, anxiety, and suicidal ideation among older married adults: Findings from a cross-sectional analysis of

the Irish Longitudinal Study on Ageing (TILDA) Journal of affective disorders 179(), 134 - 141.

99. Peter-Derex, L. (2019). Sleep and memory consolidation Neurophysiologie Clinique 49(3), 197-198.

100. Lewis, P., Knoblich, G., Poe, G. (2018). How Memory Replay in Sleep Boosts Creative Problem-Solving Trends in Cognitive Sciences 22(6), 491-503.

101. Wei, Y., Krishnan, G., Bazhenov, M. (2016). Synaptic Mechanisms of Memory Consolidation during Sleep Slow Oscillations. The Journal of neuroscience : the official journal of the Society for Neuroscience 36(15), 4231-47.

102. Palmer, C., Alfano, C. (2017). Sleep and emotion regulation: An organizing, integrative review Sleep Medicine Reviews 31(), 6-16.

103. Alhola, P., Polo-Kantola, P. (2007). Sleep deprivation: Impact on cognitive performance. Neuropsychiatric disease and treatment 3(5), 553-67.

104. Cirelli, C. (2006). Cellular consequences of sleep deprivation in the brain Sleep Medicine Reviews 10(5), 307 – 321.

105. Dai, X., Jiang, J., Zhang, Z., Nie, X., Liu, B., Pei, L., Gong, H., Hu, J., Lu, G., Zhan, Y. (2018). Plasticity and Susceptibility of Brain Morphometry Alterations to Insufficient Sleep Frontiers in Psychiatry 9(), 10761.

106. Eugene, A., Masiak, J. (2015). The Neuroprotective Aspects of Sleep. MEDtube science 3(1), 35-40.

107. Mendelsohn, A., Larrick, J. (2013). Sleep Facilitates Clearance of Metabolites from the Brain: Glymphatic Function in Aging and Neurodegenerative Diseases Rejuvenation Research 16(6), 518-523.

108. Watson, F., N., Badr, S., M., Belenky, G., Bliwise, L., D., Buxton, M., O., Buysse, D., Tasali, E., et al. (2015). Recommended amount of sleep for a healthy adult: a joint consensus state-

ment of the American Academy of Sleep Medicine and Sleep Research Society Sleep

109. Figueiro, M., Rea, M. (2010). The Effects of Red and Blue Lights on Circadian Variations in Cortisol, Alpha Amylase, and Melatonin International Journal of Endocrinology 2010(2), 1 - 9.

110. Onen, S., Onen, F., Bailly, D., Parquet, P. (1994). [Prevention and treatment of sleep disorders through regulation] of sleeping habits]. Presse médicale (Paris, France : 1983) 23(10), 485-9.

111. Koob, G., Caine, S., Hyytia, P., Markou, A., Parsons, L., Roberts, A., Schulteis, G., Weiss, F. (1999). Neurobiology of drug addiction. Drug abuse: Origins & interventions.

112. Berridge, K., Robinson, T. (1998). What is the role of dopamine in reward: hedonic impact, reward learning, or incentive salience? Brain Research Reviews 28(3), 309-369.

113. APA (2019). Data on behavioral health in the United States. [online] https:// www.apa.org. Available at: https://www.apa.org/helpcenter/data-behavioral- health

114. Nami.org. (2019). Mental Health By the Numbers | NAMI: National Alliance on Mental Illness. [online] Available at: https://www.nami.org/Learn-More/Mental-Health-By-the-Numbers

115. Schildkraut, J. (1995). The catecholamine hypothesis of affective disorders: a review of supporting evidence. 1965 [classical article] The Journal of Neuropsychiatry and Clinical Neurosciences 7(4), 524-533.

116. Hirschfeld, R. (2000). History and evolution of the monoamine hypothesis of depression. The Journal of clinical psychiatry 61 Suppl 6(), 4-6.

117. Mulinari, S. (2012). Monoamine Theories of Depression: Historical Impact on Biomedical Research Journal of the History of the Neurosciences 21(4), 366-392.

118. Dayan, P., Huys, Q. (2008). Serotonin, Inhibition, and Negative Mood PLOS Computational Biology 4(2), e4.

119. Ruhé, H., Mason, N., Schene, A. (2007). Mood is indirectly related to serotonin, norepinephrine and dopamine levels in humans: a meta-analysis of monoamine depletion studies Molecular Psychiatry 12(4), 331 - 359.

120. Fagg, G., Foster, A. (1983). Amino acid neurotransmitters and their pathways in the mammalian central nervous system Neuroscience 9(4), 701 - 719.

121. Fernstrom, J. (1977). Effects of the diet on brain neurotransmitters Metabolism 26(2), 207 - 223.

122. Yatham, L., Liddle, P., Sossi, V., Erez, J., Vafai, N., Lam, R., Blinder, S. (2012). Positron Emission Tomography Study of the Effects of Tryptophan Depletion on Brain Serotonin2 Receptors in Subjects Recently Remitted From Major Depression Archives of General Psychiatry 69(6), 601 - 609.

123. Roiser, J., McLean, A., Ogilvie, A., Blackwell, A., Bamber, D., Goodyer, I., Jones, P., Sahakian, B. (2005). The Subjective and Cognitive Effects of Acute Phenylalanine and Tyrosine Depletion in Patients Recovered from Depression Neuropsychopharmacology: official publication of the American College of Neuropsychopharmacology 30(4), 775 - 785.

124. Lodish, H., Berk, A., Zipursky, S., Matsudaira, P., Baltimore, D., Darnell, J. (2000). Neurotransmitters, Synapses, and Impulse Transmission Molecular Cell Biology. 4th edition

125. Oosterwijk, S., Lindquist, K., Anderson, E., Dautoff, R., Moriguchi, Y., Barrett, L. (2012). States of mind: Emotions, body feelings, and thoughts share distributed neural networks NeuroImage 62(3), 2110 - 2128.

126. Hyman, S. (2000). Mental Illness Genetically Complex Disorders of Neural Circuitry and Neural Communication Neuron 28(2), 321-323.

127. Akil, H., Brenner, S., Kandel, E., Kendler, K., King, M., Scolnick, E., Watson, J., Zoghbi, H. (2010). Medicine. The future of psychiatric research: genomes and neural circuits. Science (New York, N.Y.) 327(5973), 1580 - 1581.

128. George, M., Ketter, T., Post, R. (1994). Prefrontal cortex dysfunction in clinical depression Depression 2(2), 59 - 72.

129. Puig, M., Gulledge, A. (2011). Serotonin and Prefrontal Cortex Function: Neurons, Networks, and Circuits Molecular Neurobiology 44(3), 449 - 464.

130. Gorwood, P. (2008). Neurobiological mechanisms of anhedonia. Dialogues in clinical neuroscience 10(3), 291-9

131. Arco, A., Mora, F. (2009). Neurotransmitters and prefrontal cortex–limbic system interactions: implications for plasticity and psychiatric disorders Journal of Neural Transmission 116(8), 941-952.

132. Carlsson, M. (2006). A dopaminergic deficit hypothesis of schizophrenia: the path to discovery Dialogues in clinical neuroscience 8(1), 137.

133. Barnett, J., Xu, K., Heron, J., Goldman, D., Jones, P. (2011). Cognitive effects of genetic variation in monoamine neurotransmitter systems: A population-based study of COMT, MAOA, and 5HTTLPR American Journal of Medical Genetics Part B: Neuropsychiatric Genetics 156(2), 158-167.

134. Longordo, F., Kopp, C., Lüthi, A. (2009). Consequences of sleep deprivation on neurotransmitter receptor expression and function European Journal of Neuroscience 29(9), 1810-1819.

135. Fernstrom, J. (2013). Large neutral amino acids: dietary effects on brain neurochemistry and function Amino Acids 45(3), 419-430.

136. Cangiano, C., Cardelli-Cangiano, P., Cascino, A., Patrizi, M., Barberini, F., Fanelli, F., Capocaccia, L., Strom, R. (1983). On the stimulation by insulin of tryptophan transport across

the blood-brain barrier. Biochemistry international 7(5), 617-27.

137. Wurtman, R., Wurtman, J. (1986). Carbohydrate craving, obesity and brain serotonin Appetite 7(), 99-103.

138. Yamada, C., Kondo, M., Kishimoto, N., Shibata, T., Nagai, Y., Imanishi, T., Oroguchi, T., Ishii, N., Nishizaki, Y. (2015). Association between insulin resistance and plasma amino acid profile in non-diabetic Japanese subjects Journal of Diabetes Investigation 6(4), 408-415.

139. Fernstrom, J. (1990). Aromatic amino acids and monoamine synthesis in the central nervous system: influence of the diet The Journal of Nutritional Biochemistry 1(10), 508-517.

140. Zhang, M., Wen, J., Wang, X., Xiao, C. (2014). High-dose folic acid improves endothelial function by increasing tetrahydrobiopterin and decreasing homocysteine levels Molecular Medicine Reports 10(3), 1609 - 1613.

141. Kuzkaya, N., Weissmann, N., Harrison, D., Dikalov, S. (2003). Interactions of Peroxynitrite, Tetrahydrobiopterin, Ascorbic Acid, and Thiols IMPLICATIONS FORUNCOUPLING ENDOTHELIAL NITRIC-OXIDE SYNTHASE Journal of Biological Chemistry 278(25), 22546-22554.

142. Fukuwatari, T., Shibata, K. (2013). Nutritional aspect of tryptophan metabolism. International Journal of Tryptophan Research 6(Suppl 1), 3 - 8.

143. Kuhn, D., O'Callaghan, J., Juskevich, J., Lovenberg, W. (1980). Activation of brain tryptophan hydroxylase by ATP-MG2+: dependence on calmodulin Proceedings of the National Academy of Sciences 77(8), 4688 - 4691.

144. Hasegawa, H., Nakamura, K. (2010). Tryptophan Hydroxylase and Serotonin Synthesis Regulation Handbook of Behavioral Neuroscience 21(), 183 - 202.

145. Helman, G., Pappa, M., Pearl, P. (2014). JIMD Reports, Volume 17 JIMD reports 17(), 23-27.

146. Bonnefil, V., Castiglione, C., Cawthon, R., Breakefield, X. (1981). Effect of riboflavin on monoamine oxidase activity in cultured neuroblastoma cells Cellular and Molecular Neurobiology 1(4), 351-359.

147. Gaweska, H., Fitzpatrick, P. (2011). Structures and mechanism of the monoamine oxidase family BioMolecular Concepts 2(5), 365 - 377.

148. Flydal, M., Martinez, A. (2013). Phenylalanine hydroxylase: Function, structure, and regulation IUBMB Life 65(4), 341-349.

149. Swerdlow, R. (1998). Is NADH effective in the treatment of Parkinson's disease? Drugs & aging 13(4), 263 - 268.

150. Rahman, M., Rahman, F., Rahman, T., Kato, T. (2009). Dopamine-β- Hydroxylase (DBH), Its Cofactors and Other Biochemical Parameters in the Serum of Neurological Patients in Bangladesh. International journal of biomedical science: IJBS 5(4), 395-401.

151. Jeffery, D., Roth, J. (1987). Kinetic reaction mechanism for magnesium binding to membrane-bound and soluble catechol O-methyltransferase Biochemistry 26(10), 2955-2958.

152. Tsao, D., Diatchenko, L., Dokholyan, N. (2011). Structural Mechanism of S- Adenosyl Methionine Binding to Catechol O-Methyltransferase PloS one 6(8), e24287.

153. Solovyev, N. (2015). Importance of selenium and selenoprotein for brain function: From antioxidant protection to neuronal signalling Journal of Inorganic Biochemistry 153(), 1-12.

154. Doboszewska, U., Wlaź, P., Nowak, G., Radziwoń-Zaleska, M., Cui, R., Młyniec, K. (2017). Zinc in the Monoaminergic Theory of Depression: Its Relationship to Neural Plasticity. Neural plasticity 2017(6), 3682752 - 18.

155. Swardfager, W., Herrmann, N., McIntyre, R., Mazereeuw, G., Goldberger, K., Cha, D., Schwartz, Y., Lanctôt, K. (2013). Po-

tential roles of zinc in the pathophysiology and treatment of major depressive disorder. Neuroscience and biobehavioral reviews 37(5), 911 - 929.

156. Growdon, J., Wurtman, R. (1979). Brain Acetylcholine and Neuropsychiatric Disease

157. Leonardi, R., Jackowski, S. (2007). Biosynthesis of Pantothenic Acid and Coenzyme A. EcoSal Plus 2(2)

158. Shudo, K., Fukasawa, H., Nakagomi, M., Yamagata, N. (2009). Towards Retinoid Therapy for Alzheimer's Disease Current Alzheimer Research 6(3), 302- 311.

159. D, L., P, S., Davis, L., Richardson, S. (2015). Fundamentals of Neurologic Disease

160. Kidd, G., & Trapp, B. (2010). Molecular organization of the oligodendrocyte and myelin. In P.Armati & E. Mathey (Eds.), The Biology of Oligodendrocytes (pp. 64- 102). Cambridge: Cambridge University Press.

161. Saher, G., Quintes, S., Nave, K. (2011). Cholesterol: A Novel Regulatory Role in Myelin Formation The Neuroscientist 17(1), 79-93.

162. Ho, V., Lee, J., Martin, K. (2011). The Cell Biology of Synaptic Plasticity Science 334(6056), 623-628.

163. Olson, D. (2018). Psychoplastogens: A Promising Class of Plasticity-Promoting Neurotherapeutics Journal of Experimental Neuroscience 12(), 1179069518800508.

164. Valentine, R., Valentine, D. (2004). Omega-3 fatty acids in cellular membranes: a unified concept Progress in Lipid Research 43(5), 383-402.

165. Glomset, J. (2006). Role of Docosahexaenoic Acid in Neuronal Plasma Membranes Sci. STKE 2006(321), pe6-pe6.

166. Kidd, P. (2007). Omega-3 DHA and EPA for cognition, behavior, and mood: clinical findings and structural-functional synergies with cell membrane phospholipids. Alternative

medicine review : a journal of clinical therapeutic 12(3), 207-27.

167. Tanaka, K., Farooqui, A., Siddiqi, N., Alhomida, A., Ong, W. (2012). fects of Docosahexaenoic Acid on Neurotransmission Biomolecules & Therapeutics 20(2), 152-157.

168. Beard, J., Connor, J. (2003). IRON STATUS AND NEURAL FUNCTIONING dx.doi.org 23(1), 41 - 58.

169. Todorich, B., Pasquini, J., Garcia, C., Paez, P., Connor, J. (2009). Oligodendrocytes and myelination: The role of iron Glia 57(5), 467-478.

170. Herring, N., Konradi, C. (2011). Myelin copper and the cuprizone model of schizophrenia Frontiers in Bioscience S3(1), 23-40.

171. Zimmermann, M. (2011). The role of iodine in human growth and development Seminars in Cell & Developmental Biology 22(6), 645-652.

172. Martin, P., Singleton, C., Hiller-Sturmhöfel, S. (2003). The role of thiamine deficiency in alcoholic brain disease. Alcohol research & health : the journal of the National Institute on Alcohol Abuse and Alcoholism 27(2), 134-42.

173. Black, M. (2008). Effects of Vitamin B12 and Folate Deficiency on Brain Development in Children Food and Nutrition Bulletin 29(2_suppl1), S126-S131.

174. Fuente, A., Errea, O., Wijngaarden, P., Gonzalez, G., Kerninon, C., Jarjour, A., Lewis, H., Jones, C., Nait-Oumesmar, B., Zhao, C., Huang, J., ffrench-Constant, C., Franklin, R. (2015). Vitamin D receptor–retinoid X receptor heterodimer signaling regulates oligodendrocyte progenitor cell differentiation The Journal of Cell Biology 211(5), 975-985.

175. Ferland, G. (2012). Vitamin K and the Nervous System: An Overview of its Actions Advances in Nutrition: An International Review Journal 3(2), 204-212.

176. Kumar, A., Saini, R., Saini, A. (2018). NEUROPROTECTIVE ROLE OF ASCORBIC ACID: ANTIOXIDANT AND NON-ANTIOXIDANT FUNCTIONS Asian Journal of Pharmaceutical and Clinical Research 11(10), 30-33.

177. Skripuletz, T., Linker, R., Stangel, M. (2015). The choline pathway as a strategy to promote central nervous system (CNS) remyelination Neural Regeneration Research 10(9), 1369-1370.

178. Blusztajn, J., Slack, B., Mellott, T. (2017). Neuroprotective Actions of Dietary Choline Nutrients 9(8), 815.

179. Saher, G., Quintes, S., Nave, K. (2011). Cholesterol: A Novel Regulatory Role in Myelin Formation The Neuroscientist 17(1), 79-93.

180. Rich, P. (2003). The molecular machinery of Keilin's respiratory chain Biochemical Society Transactions 31(6), 1095-1105.

181. Raichle, M., Gusnard, D. (2002). Appraising the brain's energy budget Proceedings of the National Academy of Sciences 99(16), 10237-10239.

182. Magistretti, P., Allaman, I. (2015). A Cellular Perspective on Brain Energy Metabolism and Functional Imaging Neuron 86(4), 883-901.

183. Collins, A., Koechlin, E. (2012). Reasoning, Learning, and Creativity: Frontal Lobe Function and Human Decision-Making PLOS Biology 10(3), e1001293.

184. Sotres-Bayon, F., Quirk, G. (2010). Prefrontal control of fear: more than just extinction Current Opinion in Neurobiology 20(2), 231-235.

185. Cheng, A., Hou, Y., Mattson, M. (2010). Mitochondria and Neuroplasticity ASN Neuro 2(5).

186. Picard, M., McEwen, B. (2014). Mitochondria impact brain function and cognition Proceedings of the National Academy of Sciences 111(1), 7-8.

187. Sas, K., Szabó, E., Vécsei, L. (2018). Mitochondria, Oxidative Stress and the Kynurenine System, with a Focus on Ageing and Neuroprotection. Molecules (Basel, Switzerland) 23(1), 191.

188. Nunnari, J., Suomalainen, A. (2012). Mitochondria: In Sickness and in Health Cell 148(6), 1145-1159.

189. Kerner, J., Hoppel, C. (2013). Encyclopedia of Biological Chemistry (Second Edition) Metabolism Vitamins and Hormones: Article Titles: C

190. Kennedy, D. (2016). B Vitamins and the Brain: Mechanisms, Dose and Efficacy —A Review Nutrients 8(2), 68.

191. Golbidi, S., Badran, M., Laher, I. (2011). Diabetes and Alpha Lipoic Acid Frontiers in Pharmacology 2(), 69.

192. Oexle, H., Gnaiger, E., Weiss, G. (1999). Iron-dependent changes in cellular energy metabolism: influence on citric acid cycle and oxidative phosphorylation Biochimica et Biophysica Acta (BBA) - Bioenergetics 1413(3), 99-107.

193. Kurosu, M., Begari, E. (2010). Vitamin K2 in Electron Transport System: Are Enzymes Involved in Vitamin K2 Biosynthesis Promising Drug Targets? Molecules 15(3), 1531-1553.

194. Horn, D., Barrientos, A. (2008). Mitochondrial copper metabolism and delivery to cytochrome c oxidase IUBMB Life 60(7), 421-429.

195. Herculano-Houzel, S., Lent, R. (2005). Isotropic Fractionator: A Simple, Rapid Method for the Quantification of Total Cell and Neuron Numbers in the Brain The Journal of Neuroscience 25(10), 2518-2521.

196. Gehrmann, J., Matsumoto, Y., Kreutzberg, G. (1995). Microglia: Intrinsic immuneffector cell of the brain Brain Research Reviews 20(3), 269-287.

197. Block, M., Zecca, L., Hong, J. (2007). Microglia-mediated neurotoxicity: uncovering the molecular mechanisms Nature Reviews Neuroscience 8(1), 57-69.

198. Aloisi, F. (2001). Immune function of microglia Glia 36(2), 165-179.

199. Tay, T., Béchade, C., D'Andrea, I., St-Pierre, M., Henry, M., Roumier, A., Tremblay, M. (2017). Microglia Gone Rogue: Impacts on Psychiatric Disorders across the Lifespan. Frontiers in Molecular Neuroscience 10(), 421.

200. Calcia, M., Bonsall, D., Bloomfield, P., Selvaraj, S., Barichello, T., Howes, O. (2016). Stress and neuroinflammation: a systematic review of the effects of stress on microglia and the implications for mental illness Psychopharmacology 233(9), 1637 - 1650.

201. Patel, A. (2013). Review: the role of inflammation in depression. Psychiatria Danubina 25 Suppl 2(), S216-23.

202. Ates-Alagoz, Z., Adejare, A. (2013). NMDA Receptor Antagonists for Treatment of Depression Pharmaceuticals 6(4), 480-499.

203. Girgis, R., Kumar, S., Brown, A. (2014). The Cytokine Model of Schizophrenia: Emerging Therapeutic Strategies Biological Psychiatry 75(4), 292-299.

204. . Réus, G., Fries, G., Stertz, L., Badawy, M., Passos, I., Barichello, T., Kapczinski, F., Quevedo, J. (2015). The role of inflammation and microglial activation in the pathophysiology of psychiatric disorders Neuroscience 300(), 141 - 154.

205. Saijo, K., Crotti, A., Glass, C. (2013). Regulation of microglia activation and deactivation by nuclear receptors Glia 61(1), 104-111.

206. Treml, J., Šmejkal, K. (2016). Flavonoids as Potent Scavengers of Hydroxyl Radicals Comprehensive Reviews in Food Science and Food Safety 15(4), 720 - 738.

207. Kumar, S., Pandey, A. (2013). Chemistry and Biological Activities of Flavonoids: An Overview The Scientific World Journal 2013(11-12), 1 - 16.

208. Leyva-López, N., Gutierrez-Grijalva, E., Ambriz-Perez, D., Heredia, J. (2016). Flavonoids as Cytokine Modulators: A Possible Therapy for Inflammation-Related Diseases International Journal of Molecular Sciences 17(6).

209. Jang, S., reviews, R., (2010). Can consuming flavonoids restore old microglia to their youthful state? academic.oup.com

210. Kim, S. (2015). Inhibition of microglial activation and induction of neurotrophic factors by flavonoids: a potential therapeutic strategy against Parkinson's disease Neural Regeneration Research 10(3), 363-364.

211. Spagnuolo, C., Moccia, S., Russo, G. (2018). Anti-inflammatory effects of flavonoids in neurodegenerative disorders European Journal of Medicinal Chemistry 153(Expert Rev. Mol. Diagn 13 8 2013), 105-115.

212. Oliveira, L., Teixeira, F., Sato, M. (2018). Impact of Retinoic Acid on Immune Cells and Inflammatory Diseases Mediators of Inflammation 2018(), 3067126.

213. Barger, S., Goodwin, M., Porter, M., Beggs, M. (2007). Glutamate release from activated microglia requires the oxidative burst and lipid peroxidation Journal of Neurochemistry 101(5), 1205-1213.

214. Li, Y., Liu, L., Barger, S., Mrak, R., Griffin, W. (2001). Vitamin E suppression of microglial activation is neuroprotective Journal of Neuroscience Research 66(2), 163-170.

215. Mildenberger, J., Johansson, I., Sergin, I., Kjøbli, E., Damås, J., Razani, B., Flo, T., Bjørkøy, G. (2017). N-3 PUFAs induce inflammatory tolerance by formation of KEAP1-containing SQSTM1/p62-bodies and activation of NFE2L2 Autophagy 13(10), 00-00.

216. Layé, S., Nadjar, A., Joffre, C., Bazinet, R. (2018). Anti-Inflammatory Effects of Omega-3 Fatty Acids in the Brain:

Physiological Mechanisms and Relevance to Pharmacology Pharmacological Reviews 70(1), 12-38.

217. Djukic, M., Onken, M., Schütze, S., Redlich, S., Götz, A., Hanisch, U., Bertsch, T., Ribes, S., Hanenberg, A., Schneider, S., Bollheimer, C., Sieber, C., Nau, R. (2014). Vitamin D Deficiency Reduces the Immune Response, Phagocytosis Rate, and Intracellular Killing Rate of Microglial Cells Infection and Immunity 82(6), 2585- 2594.

218. Boontanrart, M., Hall, S., Spanier, J., Hayes, C., Olson, J. (2016). Vitamin D3 alters microglia immune activation by an IL-10 dependent SOCS3 mechanism Journal of Neuroimmunology 292(), 126-136.

219. Page, C., Coutellier, L. (2019). Prefrontal excitatory/inhibitory balance in stress and emotional disorders: Evidence for over-inhibition Neuroscience & Biobehavioral Reviews 105(), 39-51.

220. Marín, O. (2012). Interneuron dysfunction in psychiatric disorders Nature Reviews Neuroscience 13(2), 107-120.

221. György, B. (2006-10-26). Coupling of Systems by Oscillations. In Rhythms of the Brain. : Oxford University Press. www.xoxfordscholarship.com/view/10.1093/acprof:oso/9780195301069.001.0001/acprof 9780195301069-chapter-12

222. Gray, J. and McNaughton, N. (2008). The neuropsychology of anxiety. Oxford: Oxford University Press.

223. Wang, J., Rao, H., Wetmore, G., Furlan, P., Korczykowski, M., Dinges, D., Detre, J. (2005). Perfusion functional MRI reveals cerebral blood flow pattern under psychological stress Proceedings of the National Academy of Sciences of the United States of America 102(49), 17804-17809.

224. Ziegler, M. (2012). Primer on the Autonomic Nervous System (Third Edition) Part IV: Stress

225. Segerstrom, S., Miller, G. (2004). Psychological Stress and the Human Immune System: A Meta-Analytic Study of 30 Years of Inquiry. Psychological Bulletin 130(4), 601.

226. Cohen, S., Janicki-Deverts, D., Doyle, W., Miller, G., Frank, E., Rabin, B., Turner, R. (2012). Chronic stress, glucocorticoid receptor resistance, inflammation, and disease risk Proceedings of the National Academy of Sciences 109(16), 5995- 5999.

227. Nuss, P. (2015). Anxiety disorders and GABA neurotransmission: a disturbance of modulation. Neuropsychiatric disease and treatment 11(), 165 - 175.

228. Sohal, V., Rubenstein, J. (2019). Excitation-inhibition balance as a framework for investigating mechanisms in neuropsychiatric disorders Molecular Psychiatry 24(9), 1248-1257.

229. Simms, B., Zamponi, G. (2014). Neuronal Voltage-Gated Calcium Channels: Structure, Function, and Dysfunction Neuron 82(1), 24-45.

230. Albrecht, J., Sidoryk-Węgrzynowicz, M., Zielińska, M., Aschner, M. (2010). Roles of glutamine in neurotransmission. Neuron glia biology 6(4), 263-76.

231. Nicoll, R. (2017). A Brief History of Long-Term Potentiation Neuron 93(2), 281- 290.

232. Huang, Y., Su, L., Wu, J. (2016). Pyridoxine Supplementation Improves the Activity of Recombinant Glutamate Decarboxylase and the Enzymatic Production of Gama-Aminobutyric Acid. PloS one 11(7), e0157466.

233. Branchereau, P., Cattaert, D., Delpy, A., Allain, A., Martin, E., Meyrand, P. (2016). Depolarizing GABA/glycine synaptic events switch from excitation to inhibition during frequency increases Scientific Reports 6(1), 21753.

234. Wu, J., Prentice, H. (2010). Role of taurine in the central nervous system Journal of Biomedical Science 17(Suppl 1), S1

235. Johnson, J., Ascher, P. (1990). Voltage-dependent block by intracellular Mg2+ of N-methyl-D-aspartate-activated channels Biophysical Journal 57(5), 1085-1090.

236. Ruppersberg, J., Kitzing, E., Schoepfer, R. (1994). The mechanism of magnesium block of NMDA Seminars in Neuroscience 6(2), 87-96.

237. Mlyniec, K. (2015). Zinc in the Glutamatergic Theory of Depression Current Neuropharmacology 13(4), 505-513.

CPSIA information can be obtained
at www.ICGtesting.com
Printed in the USA
FSHW021248021020
74395FS